D0731040

CONTENTS

For information write: Vocational Publishing
10620 Fillmore St.
N.E., Blaine, MN   55434.

DEPARTURE: START WITH THE KEY

The key to a successful job search is **research** and **preparation**. You must research the companies you wish to work for and prepare yourself for the employment maze you are about to enter. This book will help you streamline your background and qualifications in order to impress a potential employer with your capabilities. However, you must supply the three D's: determination, desire, and dedication. It takes all three to discover the job meant for **YOU**.

FIRE UP

One of the most difficult aspects of the job search is learning to maintain a positive attitude about yourself and your skills in the face of employer rejection. In any sales position (and this is the ultimate sales position you will ever encounter) three basics must be followed: 1) Make the contact, 2) Make an enthusiastic presentation (interest the buyer), and 3) Close the sale. A good salesperson knows that every rejection ultimately brings one closer to success. Valuable experience, information, and future contacts can be realized from each "sales presentation."

REGULATOR

Approach your job hunt as if it were a full time job itself. If you are out of work (and school) use your days as if you were scheduled to put in a full day on the job. It is important to keep a regular schedule. This will help to keep you from feeling depressed. Get up in the morning, get dressed, and get going on getting the job you want! This is essential to giving yourself a sense of purpose and committment.

CONTACT POINTS

Split your days into various work tasks:

8 to 10 . . . . phone calling

10 to 10:30 . . . . break time

10:30 to 12 . . . . update paper work

12 to 1 . . . . lunch date*

1 to 4 . . . . make in person contact: informational interviews, job interviews, follow up on past interviews, continue library research, drop resumes off to prospective employers, visit past employers or school placement offices, check in with private or state employment services.

*It is important to maintain contact with the outside world to keep updated about trends in your field and to help you maintain a positive attitude about yourself.

FUEL ECONOMY

The point is: if you let your engine idle all day, you will eventually run out of gas and still be at the starting line. **DO ANYTHING EXCEPT IDLE AROUND AND SPUTTER ABOUT THE FACT THAT YOU DON'T HAVE A JOB!**

CHARACTER ASSESSMENT

PRODUCT ANALYSIS

In order to present yourself in the best way to a potential employer you must become aware of all aspects of your background that lend themselves to the employment setting. You must understand what skills you have to offer — both technical and personal.

PARTS LIST

Review this list of personal attributes. Check those that describe you.

imaginative	friendly	assertive
curious	cheerful	enthusiastic
thoughtful	straightforward	hard worker
open	witty	love a challenge
honest	cautious	loyal
motivated	neat	easy-going
team worker	modest	energetic
leader	persuasive	methodical
supportive	verbal	careful
sympathetic	quiet	precise
understanding	happy	quick learner
eager	serious	diplomatic
adventurous	dedicated	competitive
risk-taker	practical	cooperative
persistent	resourceful	mediator
dependable	problem solver	conscientious
reliable	creative	independent
flexible	artistic	high achiever

U-TURN AND CIRCLE the five traits that you feel are your strongest assets in a working environment. You should highlight these traits throughout the employment process.

If one of your best friends were describing you, what personal characteristics would he/she mention?

If a teacher were describing you, what personal characteristics would he/she mention?

Are there some personal characteristics that you need to develop which would help you become more successful in acquiring and keeping a job? List them.

CHECK YOUR TOOL BOX

Gathering information and networking (gathering contacts) are important job search tools. Research involves: knowing the nature of your work, knowing the industry surrounding it (library research), knowing as much as possible about the specific company in which you are interested (informational interviewing), and acquiring contacts within an organization or industry (networking).

ASKING NATIVES FOR DIRECTIONS

The practice of gathering career information from people working in areas of your interest is a primary job hunt strategy. Informational interviewing is one way to research a company that you are interested in working for. However, before arriving at an informational interview, it would be beneficial to have gained as much background as possible from other resources, i.e., the library, friends who work there, relatives, observation (if possible), teachers, customers, former employees; any imaginable source available to you. The main purposes of informational interviewing are:

1) To develop a network of contacts

2) To learn about an organization from the inside

3) To practice interviewing in a non-threatening environment

Do not expect informational interviews to result in immediate job offers. Just learn as much as you can about the person you are interviewing and the organization they work for as well as the industry as a whole (as they see it). When you are ready to start your job search in earnest, contact the people you met through informational interviews and ask for help in developing job leads.

CAR POOLING

Networking is based on the assumption that everyone you know is a channel to someone else, and eventually you will get to a person who is in a position to help you further your career goals. Networking is a life long process and does not end once you are gainfully employed. Using personal contacts is one of the most efficient ways of gaining access to information concerning your job goal.

Start by contacting five people you know. Ask each for a referral pertinent to your job search. The five people can be friends, relatives, former employers, teachers, etc. Everyone knows someone who in turn may know someone who knows a person in the hiring seat. This chain of people becomes your network pool.

Don't forget to join and become active in your professional trade association. This provides an excellent vehicle for making contacts. The resources you gather through networking will help you set up informational interviews. Using someone's name by way of introduction helps establish a rapport that makes it easier to set up an interview.

Another way to set up informational interviews with employers is to state that you are a student studying _____ and have a school project to complete on _____. Ask if they could schedule some time to answer a few questions. It helps to tell them that you heard they have expertise in your field of interest. This technique also works for investigating career choices if you are not sure which one is right for you.

TURN ON YOUR SPOTLIGHT

Identify a company that hires people with your background and training. Research this company as thoroughly as possible. Attempt to locate someone who can refer you to someone who works there. Set up an informational interview. It is best to meet in the person's work environment if possible.

PLAN YOUR ROUTE:

Before you go to the interview, draw up a list of questions that will provide information about how the company functions and about future job prospects.

KNOW WHAT TO ASK

The following questions are suggestions: add or streamline to meet your personal needs.

1) What is your job title?
2) Specifically, what do you do in your work? What are your responsibilities on a typical day?
3) How did you get into this field of work? What was your background and training? What helped you the most in attaining your current position?
4) What are the current qualifications for an entry level position in this field within your company?
5) What are the typical salary ranges for entry-level positions in this field?
6) What is your prediction regarding the employment outlook in this field? in this company?
7) Do you know any other people in this field (or company) that you think could offer some advice on career strategies? MAKE SURE YOU GET A NAME AND ASK IF YOU CAN USE THIS PERSON'S NAME AS THE REFERRAL SOURCE.
8) Are there any other resources that you could recommend to me such as: books, professional organizations, seminars, etc.
9) Can you suggest any related occupations that I might investigate?

IT IS PERMISSIBLE TO TAKE NOTES DURING THE INTERVIEW; IT IS FLATTERING.

LUBRICATION

To keep things running smoothly, after conducting informational interviews *always* send a thank you note expressing your appreciation for the interviewer's time, interest, and information.

CAUTION

Some employers are highly skeptical of informational interviews. Be careful not to ask for a job after you have made information your prime objective for meeting with an employer. No one likes to feel that they have been deceived. It is best to conduct informational interviews while you are receiving your training and before you are actively seeking employment. After graduation you can "drop off" a copy of your resume and inform the employer that you are looking for a job. You may get some good job leads.

DIAGNOSTIC ANALYSIS REPORT FORM

_____

STUDENT NAME

_____

CAREER AREA

_____

INSTRUCTOR

Please fill in the information requested:

NAME OF PERSON INTERVIEWED _____

HIS/HER TITLE _____

COMPANY NAME _____

WORK PHONE NUMBER _____

DATE OF INTERVIEW _____

DATE OF THANK YOU NOTE _____

PERSON'S JOB DESCRIPTION _____

_____

_____

WHAT ARE THE ADVANTAGES OF WORKING FOR THIS FIRM_____

_____

_____

DISADVANTAGES_____

_____

WHO HIRES EMPLOYEES IN THE DEPARTMENT YOU ARE INTERESTED IN

_____ HIS/HER TITLE _____

WHAT FURTHER RESOURCES WERE YOU GIVEN _____

_____

_____

_____

_____

MAPS, CHARTS, AND DIRECTIONS

NEWSPAPERS

Newspapers (local, metropolitan, and national) are one of the most widely used methods for advertising employment openings. Newspapers are a good starting point when looking for job leads. You can find these job leads in the "Help Wanted" section (better known as the classified section) of the paper. The jobs are listed alphabetically by title. Your area of interest will probably be listed under more than one job title. When using the want ads:

1) Read the entire section(s) that applies to your field.

2) Note the size of the ads, the salary ranges, the number of job listings and the job locations.

3) Keep a list of the jobs that seemed interesting.

4) Save the advertisement for reference.

Although most job seekers use the want ads only when seeking employment, the resourceful applicant uses them for research and resources. Don't limit your search and research to the help wanted section of the paper. Read (and clip) any article about companies that employ people with your skills. You may be able to discover job openings before your competition does.

PROFESSIONAL ASSOCIATIONS AND TRADE PUBLICATIONS

Almost every field has a professional association which is organized to meet the needs of the people employed in that specialty. In order to find associations related to your field, check the Encyclopedia of Associations which lists 1,400 groups. Another source is the Scientific and Technical Societies Institutions of the U.S. and Canada, or check the yellow pages of the telephone directory under the title "Associations and Professional Organizations." Many professional associations publish newsletters or magazines which provide updated information concerning their field.

Find out how to join the association affiliated with your field and ask to be put on their mailing list. Often, the association people you contact may know of potential job openings, company expansions, or new businesses opening up in the area. LET THEM KNOW THAT YOU ARE LOOKING FOR A JOB.

Some trade publications contain their own classified sections which advertise job openings. The ads are usually placed in the back section of most magazines and newsletters. Also, look for announcements of professional meetings, conventions, seminars, and conferences that are scheduled for your area in the near future. Make an attempt to attend these events — they will provide a fertile arena to contact potential employers in person.

LIBRARY

Your school library should have an excellent assortment of publications and books concerning technological advances in business. It will also contain reference indexes to local companies and organizations. Visit the business section of any public library for reference works that list the names of local companies and the names of people who work there that have the power to hire you. Librarians are very helpful; they can help you locate and research companies of interest to you.

TOLLWAY . . . PRIVATE EMPLOYMENT AGENCIES

Private employment agencies match workers with job openings. They contact and setup interviews with employers for you. They can provide inside information to you about the company and the person who will be interviewing you. They will "sell" you to a prospective employer. They will charge a fee (MONEY) if they find you an acceptable job. No fee is charged if you do NOT accept a job offer. THEY ARE IN BUSINESS TO MAKE MONEY. Their primary function is to "sell" jobs to applicants and applicants to employers. They are NOT social service agencies.

Approach an interview with an employment agency in the same manner that you would an employer. You will have to fill out an application blank and sign a contract. The contract lists what it will cost if the agency finds a job for you. Before you sign it make sure you understand what it says. Any time you sign a legal document you are agreeing to everything it says. It is okay to change a contract if both parties agree to the change. Any change should be made in ink and initialed by all parties (people) involved.

The most frequent change made on employment agency contracts is to add "WILL ACCEPT FEE PAID ONLY." This means that the job seeker will only go on interviews where the employer has agreed to pay the "fee" for the person they hire. The disadvantage of adding this clause to the contract is that it will limit the number of job interviews you can be sent on. Other ways fees are paid include:

1) APPLICANT PAID — you pay.

2) SPLIT — you and the employer split the cost.

3) REIMBURSE — you pay and after a period of time (usually a year) the employer pays you back if you are still working.

4) NEGOTIABLE — the employer is willing to discuss who pays.

There are some advantages to using an employment agency. They may know of a job opening of which you would not be aware. The agency can provide you with feedback on how well you did at the interview. The employment service will "coach" you for the interview and actively "sell" you to the employer.

FREEWAY . . . PUBLIC EMPLOYMENT SERVICE

State Employment Services are a free public service available to employers and job seekers. Employers can call any State Employment Office to list a current job opening. After you fill out an application blank you will meet with a "counselor" who attempts to match you with a job opening on file for which you are qualified. Like a private agency, they will set up the interview appointment for you. Unlike private agencies, the state does not actively recruit jobs for you or for their job bank system. Also, the public service will not "sell" you as much as a private agency does. Employers with job openings may use this service if they wish but they are not required to use it. The big advantage of this service is that it is FREE!

TRAVEL INFORMATION CENTER

JOB BANK SYSTEM

The job bank system (micro-fiche viewer) is part of the state job service. To use the job bank system:

1) Locate the micro-fiche viewer (looks like a small TV screen).

2) Find the job codes list.

3) Locate the job code for your field.

4) Select the micro-fiche that lists your job code(s).

5) Remove the micro-fiche from envelope and place on view finder.

6) Search micro-fiche until you find your code listings.

7) Write down any job listings you are interested in.

8) Make an appointment with the placement counselor to find out the name and address of the company.

9) Usually, the placement counselor will call the employer for you to arrange an interview time and date.

MISCELLANEOUS RESOURCES

WAYSIDE CHAPEL

Check with churches. Often local clergy are aware of employment possibilities. Leave your resume.

CONSTRUCTION ZONE

Visit work sites. It is a good idea to visit work sites in progress to ask if there will be any job openings available when the business is operating.

USE YOUR REAR VIEW MIRROR

Talk with former employers. If you left a job in good standing, contact your former bosses to see if they know of any openings in the community.

COMBUSTION CHAMBER

Visit the chamber of commerce. They may be aware of new companies locating in the area.

SLOW MOVING TRAFFIC: BE PATIENT

GOVERNMENT OFFICES — FEDERAL, STATE, AND LOCAL

The federal government is the largest employer in the nation. In applying you will have to fill out an application. Later you will be called to take a test. The people who place highest on the test will be called for an interview. Your name will go on a list if you place in the top one hundred applications. You can be called in the future as job openings occur. In general, it will take more time to get a government job than a job in the private sector. For further information concerning job openings that you may qualify for, contact any of the numbers listed below. You can request to be put on a mailing list.

MOTOR CLUB MEMBERSHIP APPLICATION

Nearly all employers use some form of an application blank. Not all application blanks are the same; some are short and simple, some are long and complex. In completing an application for employment you should:

1) Read through the application completely before you answer any questions (ask questions if necessary).

2) Print or write clearly. Use a pen.

3) Use words you know how to spell. All spelling must be correct.

4) Be complete. Don't skip or omit lines. If there is a question you do not wish to answer—draw a line in the space. If a question does not apply to you, write NA (not applicable) or none.

5) FOLLOW THE DIRECTIONS exactly as they are given. Notice if you should fill in the blanks above or below the lines.

DRIVING RECORD
INFORMATION TO BRING WITH YOU:

1. Social Security Number.

2. Present address. The employer may ask how long you have lived there.

3. Previous address. If it is the same as #2 you may write: SAME AS ABOVE.

4. Educational Background. Complete address and dates of attendance.

5. Work History. Job title, company name and mailing address, dates employed, job duties, supervisor, salary, and reason for leaving.

6. References. Name, occupation, mailing address, phone number, and your relationship to that person.

ADDITIONAL INSURANCE

*Purchase and bring a NEW ink pen with you so that you don't have to switch in the middle of the process.

*Specify the job title you want to apply for . . . if several could be interesting to you, list them all. Do NOT leave this space blank or write "anything" or "open".

*For rate of pay expected put "open" or "negotiable". Salary is one of the primary negotiable items in an interview and should be used that way.

*Think carefully about the reasons for leaving work. Respond as posivitely as you can, i.e., "advancement," "better opportunity," "more challenging work," "to enter career field," etc.

*Sign your application. By signing the application form you are giving the employer the right to check your facts. BE HONEST.

BILL BOARDS

ADVERTISING: LOOKING GOOD ON PAPER

When seeking employment you are actually in the business of selling yourself. To do the best selling job, you must advertise in writing. To stimulate the interest of an employer you must highlight the sparkle in your new paint job. List all the extras that go with your standard equipment. Be specific. Let the employer see that you are a finely tuned machine capable of performing the job. Sometimes a one page advertisement is called a flyer; for a job seeker it is known as a RESUME.

A resume serves several important functions: 1) Interests an employer in interviewing you, 2) helps to tailor the interview, and 3) serves as a reminder of your qualifications after the interview is over.

Resume writing is a tough task. The following general suggestions are offered as a guide to writing a better resume.

PLAN SHORTEST ROUTE

No resume needs to be longer than two pages and the preferred length is one page.

KNOW YOUR DESTINATION

Tailor your resume to the kind of job you are seeking; if you have more than one job objective you will need to write more than one resume — one for each type of job you want.

KEEP MOVING FORWARD

Emphasize only your positive points. Put your best qualifications at or near the top of the resume. Spell out your responsibilities emphasizing your accomplishments. Never put anything negative on your resume that might cause you to be screened out.

OBEY TRAFFIC LAWS

Be honest. Don't exaggerate or misrepresent yourself. A high percentage of employers verify the information given on a resume.

EQUIPMENT SPECIFICATIONS

Be specific. Prospective employers want to know what you can do for them. Describing what you have done in the past gives them a good idea. State the type of products (brand name) you have used, specify the equipment you can operate, processes involved, etc.

SOUND HORN

Write in clear, concise language. Use simple terms rather than complex expressions. Use active verbs (action words). Clauses that start with a verb are better than sentences. Avoid using the personal pronoun "I."

DO NOT CROSS WHITE LINE

Be neat. Make no typographical errors. Spell correctly and use appropriate punctuation.

SCENIC OVERLOOK

Make it look good. Use a standard size (8½ by 11) quality bond paper. Keep the color business like (white, eggshell, grey, beige). Use a black typewriter ribbon and make sure the typewriter elements are clean. Your resume needs to be visually attractive to the reader.

APPLY POLISH AND BUFF

Professionally reproduce your resume so that all copies resemble the original. An off-set printer will (for a small fee) use bold face type for headings and add a border if you want.

GAS, FOOD, & LODGING

The body of your resume has three basic sections: 1) your educational background and skills, 2) your work experience, and 3) your personal background and attributes. These basic sections can be broken down into a variety of sub-headings:

THE ROAD HOME

HEADING................................ your name, mailing address, city, state, zip code, and your phone number (include area code).

Placed near top of page; usually centered

SUSPENSION SYSTEM

JOB OBJECTIVE......................... summarize in one or two sentences the *specific* position you want, type and size of company, and a reason why an employer might be interested in you.

Usually placed 2nd; may sometimes precede heading or be omitted.

EXAMPLES: Press operator in a medium-sized printing company where ability to meet deadlines and operate a variety of presses would prove useful.

or

GRAPHIC ARTIST: offering experience in all areas of production printing from typesetting of copy through press runs. Special skills include silk-screening and keylining.

SCHOOL ZONE

EDUCATION .... for most vocational students this section offers the greatest potential for impressing an employer. Show your most relevant training first. Include academic awards or grade point average if it's impressive. You can also list related training. Do not put the year you graduated from high school if your age would prove detrimental. Simply state: graduate.

Can be sub-divided into:
trade/vocational
college
high school/general
if desired.

DISPLAY TRAINING PATCHES

TECHNICAL SKILLS.......................

Can be placed before or after education block.

List specific equipment you can operate; processes you can perform and technical techniques with which you are familiar. Trade jargon can be used here. Coordinate this category with your job objective.

SERVICE RECORD

EMPLOYMENT HISTORY.................

*Place first **if** you have significant work experience related to your job objective. Must give dates of employment (mo. & yr. to mo. & yr.), name of company, and position title. May include mailing address, supervisors name, and ph. #.*

Present in reverse chronological order (most current job first). Stress accomplishments and measurable results. Mention numbers and figures. Include supervisory experience, number of employees supervised, and promotions received. Use action words*; communicate that you are a doer!

EXAMPLES: Handled receipts in excess of $6,000 daily.

Performed 6 oil changes per hour.

Revamped filing system for sales and marketing departments.

Exceeded production quotas; assembled 6 face frames per hour.

Handled monthly operating budget of $20,000.

Trained, scheduled and supervised 6 employees during night shift.

CLOVER LEAF

PERSONAL REMARKS....................

Usually placed at the end of a resume. A personal character summary may also be included in this section.

All positive job related information that reflects favorably on your employability. Use clauses which start with active verbs*. Stress your personal strengths; support with facts.

*see sign posts on page 27

HIT THE BRAKES
MILITARY EXPERIENCE . . . .
Place lower on page or on 2nd page if two page resume.

Unless this experience is directly related to your career or adds to your qualifications, it is sufficient to list dates of service, branch, occupation specialty, and type of discharge.

EXTRA GEARS
ALTERNATIVES . . . .

You can begin your resume with a category called QUALIFICATIONS or CAPABILITIES. Your qualifications should relate directly to your job objective.

An ACHIEVEMENTS/AWARDS CATEGORY could substitute for the personal remarks section.

Include an ASSOCIATIONS/AC-TIVITIES category if it will show community involvement or leadership abilities.

SIGN POSTS

actively	participated
analyzed	performed
arranged	prepared
built	presented
completed	proficient at
conducted	provided
coordinated	repaired
created	responsible
demonstrated	restored
designed	revised
developed	scheduled
distributed	set up
examined	solved
improved	strengthened
increased	studied
led	successfully
maintained	supervised
organized	trained

ACTION WORDS THAT HELP TO CREATE A POSITIVE PICTURE

DON'T BE A LITTERBUG!

OMIT THESE ITEMS FROM YOUR RESUME

REFERENCES
WARNING TICKET

State "references available on request" at the bottom of your resume. You may prepare a separate sheet listing your references to hand the employer at the interview if you wish.

REASONS FOR LEAVING PAST JOBS
$200 FINE

Should not be written. May be discussed at the interview.

SALARY REQUIREMENTS
$500 FINE

It is best to negotiate salary with the employer directly. This usually occurs at the second interview.

PHOTOGRAPHS
30 DAYS HARD LABOR

Sending a picture of yourself is an outdated practice. Pictures were requested in the past in order to discriminate.

HOBBIES
LIFE WITHOUT PAROLE

Do not include hobbies or social interests unless they contribute to your work abilities.

PERSONAL DATA
DEATH ROW

Do not list marital status, race, religion, height, weight, number of children, or age.

LANDSCAPE

LAYOUT AND DESIGN: MAKE IT LOOK GOOD The first impression a resume gives may predict whether or not it is even read. How your resume appears is very important.

WATCH FOR POTHOLES AND FALLEN ROCKS

Consider how margins, headings, capital letters, spacing, and underlining can be used to give a sense of organization, orderliness, readability, and neatness.

Cut and paste. Experiment with various layouts until you discover what is pleasing to the eye. The layout should enhance the content drawing attention to your strongest selling points. PLACEMENT = EMPHASIS.

Type a clean and errorless resume. If you don't have the skill — hire it done.

Make sure that your information is balanced on the page, both vertically and horizontally. White space adds emphasis. A simple border and/or bold face type are other design techniques which can add appeal to your resume.

Have your resume professionally reproduced. Pick a quality bond paper and ask the printer to supply you with matching envelopes and 2nd sheets so that your cover letters will match your resume.

TURN ON BACK-UP-LIGHTS

Study MANY different resume examples (whether they relate to your field or not) to assess their strengths. **Take notes** on word choice, layout & design, etc. Determine what makes them good. Use what you've learned to create your own resume; add the sparkle that is uniquely you. NOTE: Most people produce boring resumes because they model theirs after only one textbook example. Even good models become boring if an employer sees them over and over again.   **NOTE: See Appendix A for Resume Examples**

heading {
_____
_____
_____
_____

CAREER OBJECTIVE

_____
_____

QUALIFICATIONS

- _____   - _____   - _____
- _____   - _____   - _____
- _____   - _____   - _____

EDUCATION

(Name of School)   Majored in:_____
(Mailing address)   Grade Point Average_____
(City, state zip)

(Name of School)   Majored in:_____
(Mailing address)   Grade Point Average_____
(City, state zip)

EMPLOYMENT HISTORY

___(company name)___,___(address)___,___(city, state zip)

Employed from_____to_____Position:_____
         (accomplishments/responsibilities)
         (transferable skills gained)

___(company name)___,___(address)___,___(city, state zip)

Employed from_____to_____Position:_____
         (accomplishments/responsibilities)
         (transferable skills gained)

CHARACTER ATTRIBUTES

- _____   - _____   - _____
- _____   - _____   - _____

References and transcripts available upon request

28

heading {
_____
_____
_____
_____

OBJECTIVE
_____
_____
_____

TRADE EDUCATION
(Name of School)
(Address)
(City, state   zip)

Major area:_____
                Graduated:_____

EQUIPMENT EXPERIENCE
• _____   • _____
• _____   • _____
• _____   • _____

RELATED TRAINING
_____
_____
_____

EMPLOYMENT HISTORY

Dates
(Name of company, city, state   zip)
(Position title and job description)

Dates
(Name of company, city, state   zip)
(Position title and job description)

Dates
(Name of company, city, state   zip)
(Position title and job description)

Dates
(Name of company, city, state   zip)
(Position title and job description)

PERSONAL REMARKS
_____
_____
_____

TRANSCRIPTS AND REFERENCES AVAILABLE ON REQUEST

WRITE FOR RESERVATIONS

A letter of application (cover letter) adds to the resume by summarizing the potential value of the applicant. The cover letter should focus on meeting the needs of a specific job and serves as a request for a job interview. There are three general uses for a letter of application:

1) As a cover letter when mailing resumes.
2) When answering an advertisement.
3) When you wish to contact an employer who lives in another city.

Cover letters, unlike resumes, are usually individually written and typed. Your letter should make the employer want to review your resume and then to interview you.

In responding to a specific job opening, you should take time to identify the employer's needs accurately. In order to write a successful cover letter, ask yourself the following questions:

1) WHAT ARE THE GOALS OF THIS EMPLOYER?

2) HOW DO THESE GOALS RELATE TO ME?

3) WHAT DO I HAVE IN COMMON WITH THE EMPLOYER?

From this information you can begin to plan the best strategy for your application letter.

WARNING — DANGER ZONE

If your letter contains errors, it becomes a liability instead of an asset. Since an application letter and resume precede the personal interview (giving the first impression of you to the employer), they should be neat, clean, and mechanically flawless. Do NOT make grammatical, spelling, or typographical errors. Employers screen out letters and resumes that are sloppy or inaccurate or that contain mechanical errors, especially when many people are applying for the same job.

BASIC COVER LETTER FORMAT

	RETURN ADDRESS:	street address
		city, state zip
	(single space)	date of letter

(space 4-6 lines)

INSIDE ADDRESS:
all lines flush to left hand margin

name of person to whom you are writing
person's title
company name
street address
city, state zip

(double space)

SALUTATION;

Dear Ms. or Mr. So and So: (use colon:)

(double space)

PARAGRAPH ONE:

State why you are writing and how you learned about the job opening. Be specific.

(double space)

PARAGRAPH TWO:
May extend into two paragraphs

Stress your individual qualifications and how they meet the needs of the employer. Toot your own horn — but softly. Refer to enclosed resume.

(double space)

CLOSING PARAGRAPH

Call to action. Ask for an interview. State when you will contact the employer to set up a specific interview time and date. This technique emphasizes your serious interest and gives you a way to learn if the company is interested in meeting you. Examples to follow.

COMPLIMENTARY CLOSE

(double space)

Sincerely,

(4 spaces)
align with return address

(your signature)

Type your name

(double space)

ENCLOSURE NOTATION

Enclosure
(at left hand margin)

HUB CAPS — CHROME PLATED

INTRODUCTORY PARAGRAPH EXAMPLES:

After reading your advertisement for a cabinetmaker in the <u>St. Paul Dispatch</u>, I feel qualified to apply for . . .

Mr. Adair, a machine shop instructor at St. Paul TVI, suggested I contact you regarding your current opening for an experienced machinist. I am confident that I can perform the machining tasks necessary.

In a recent advertisement your organization emphasized a desire to hire a person with training and experience in commercial art. Since my training and freelance experience directly relate to your job needs I wish to be considered for . . .

CLOSING PARAGRAPH EXAMPLES:

If you are interested in my qualifications for your tool and die opening, I will be available anytime next week to meet with you in person to discuss employment possibilities. I will call you Tuesday morning to arrange an interview time and date convenient to us both.

I look forward to getting together to discuss your current job opening in the art preparation department. I will call you during the early part of next week, January 14, to arrange an interview time and date. I look forward to discussing my possible involvement with 3M.

Although my personal data sheet contains considerable detail, you no doubt have questions you want answered. I will be contacting you in the near future to set up an agreeable appointment time and date. Thank you for your consideration.

I am confident that I would be an asset to your salon. I am eager to practice my technical and creative skills in a well known salon such as yours. Since I live very close to your shop meeting with you in the early part of next week can be easily managed. I will contact you on Monday to arrange a time convenient to your appointment schedule.

NOTE: See Appendix B for Cover letter Examples

THE TRAVELER'S CHECKLIST

1. Type neatly, using care in sentence structure, spelling, punctuation, and grammar.

2. Use a good grade of letter size (8½ by 11) bond paper. (Should match the resume).

3. Address your letter to a specific person. This shows that you have done your homework.

4. Be clear, brief, and businesslike.

5. Keep a copy of your letter to use for proper follow-up. Record on the letter the progress made and the days of subsequent events.

6. Always send a copy of your resume with your cover letter.

7. It is the job seeker's responsibility to contact the potential employer to arrange an interview time and date.

8. It is best to send letters/resumes to people you have already talked to. See informational interviewing and networking sections.

9. Tailor the cover letter to fit the particular job opening.

10. DON'T LET QUALIFICATIONS LISTED IN AN AD STOP YOU FROM APPLYING IF YOU DON'T MEET THEM EXACTLY. GO FOR IT ANYWAY!

WHERE THE RUBBER MEETS THE ROAD

CHECK LIST FOR PERSONAL JOB INTERVIEW:

1. Learn as much as possible about the company and the job before the interview.

2. Know about yourself and your career.

3. Present essential information about your qualifications.

4. Answer questions clearly and courteously.

5. Ask relevant questions.

A job interview is a question and answer session about you, the available job, and the company. It is a two way street.

NAME, RANK, AND HORSEPOWER

Interviewers evalute applicants with respect to two basic categories: **QUALIFICATIONS** and **PERSONAL ATTRIBUTES.** They weigh intangible factors such as personality traits, ideals and attitudes, along with basic education and work experience. The interview can be a nerve-racking experience for the job seeker who does not know what to expect. The job seeker who understands the function of the interview and prepares for this meeting in advance can use the interview to advantage.

FACTORS EMPLOYERS ARE LOOKING FOR:

1. Experience for the job.

2. Knowledge for the job.

3. Skills for the job.

4. Stability of applicant.

5. Work reliability
   a) absenteeism
   b) work attitude

6. Sincere desire for the job.

7. The person "fits" the company style.

TUNE UP

In order to be successful you must PREPARE for the interview. Know what you have to offer a company. You need to know what your goals are in order to project a responsible image. The basic principle of interviewing is to learn to anticipate what will probably occur. THE PERSON WHO GETS HIRED IS NOT NECESSARILY THE PERSON WHO CAN DO THE BEST JOB OR IS THE MOST SKILLED, BUT THE ONE WHO KNOWS THE MOST ABOUT GETTING HIRED.

DON'T GO WITH A DEAD BATTERY . . .

In an interview be enthusiastic. Show that you really want to work. As important as what you say, is how you say it: your posture, tone of voice, etc.

STAY ACCIDENT FREE . . .

Most interviewers are looking for more than mere answers to their questions. They are trying to determine if you are perceptive and can think on your feet. They are measuring your initiative, maturity, attitude, and communication skills. NEVER CRITICIZE FORMER EMPLOYERS, WORK SITES, CO-WORKERS, OR TEACHERS.

STANDARD ACCESSORIES

PERSONALITY TRAITS LOOKED FOR AND EVALUATED IN AN INTERVIEW

Stability

Persistence

Self-reliance

Patience

Reliability

Co-operativeness

Loyalty

Honesty

Competitiveness

Maturity

LOG BOOK

Your answers to interview questions asked should be logical, clearly stated, brief, and truthful, as well as spoken with enthusiasm and confidence. You need to EMPHASIZE THE POSITIVE! If, for example, the interviewer asks, "Tell me about yourself." Your answer should stress your training, your skills, your additional work experience, and any accomplishments that would qualify you for the job opening.

Don't underestimate the value of work experience. Any work experience is of interest to an employer because it indicates that you can carry out instructions and are reliable.

CAR WASH

While it may seem superficial, people are influenced by your appearance. Especially if they are considering hiring you. A thirty minute interview is a short time to make a good impression. You need to get off on the right foot by being well groomed and appropriately dressed. Different jobs call for different standards of dress, but a good rule to follow is to be as well dressed as your interviewer.

HEADREST

Most people are a bit nervous before an interview. It helps to remember that interviewers are looking for people to hire; they are not out to get you. A skilled interviewer will usually help a nervous applicant overcome this problem.

REVIEW TRAVEL PLANS

The interview is usually broken into three distinct parts:

1.   *The interviewer asks the applicant questions.*

2.   *The interviewer briefly describes the job and the company.*

3.   *The applicant asks the interviewer questions.*

To create a good impression, don't answer questions with a simple yes or no; be informative without boasting or telling your troubles. Listening and the ability to ask appropriate questions are related interviewing skills. Listening carefully and asking questions when you are not sure you understand the interviewer's question makes a good impression at job interviews. It is a good idea to politely ask the interviewer to rephrase or repeat a question if you are confused.

When you are talking to an interviewer, be honest. When you are asked what your weaknesses in a work situation might be, don't say you can't think of any. That sounds conceited and boastful. Most employers want their employees to be able to recognize their individual weaknesses so that they can work on improving them. People who have no limitations are not able to improve their performance.

Asking the interviewer questions shows that you are interested in the company and the position for which you are applying. Prepare questions of interest to you to take with you to the interview. It is permissible to refer to your notes during this stage of the interview. Also, if the interviewer failed to give you an opportunity to present your strengths you can preface your questions with your strengths and inquire if the position calls for someone with those abilities.

DUAL EXHAUST

There are two main categories of questions commonly used by interviewers: closed and open ended questions. The closed question is a direct request for information.

"Where did you go to school?"

"Are you looking for a full time job?"

"When would you be able to start work?"

These questions will help you relax into a natural conversation while supplying the interviewer with relevant information. Answer closed questions directly and briefly.

The open ended question is meant to shift the interview into areas of attitudes and personal characteristics.

"What are your future goals?"

"What type of boss do you like?"

"What have you learned from the jobs you have held?"

"Tell me about yourself."

These questions are more difficult to answer. Take your time in answering them and explain your response completely. Always think before you answer. These types of questions help the employer to determine what kind of person you are and therefore what kind of employee you would be.

It is possible that you may be asked how much you want to be paid. The usual answer when you are first establishing yourself in a career, is to indicate you are more interested in a job where you can prove yourself and improve your skills than you are in a specific salary. This politely passes the question back to the interviewer. If the employer pursues the matter, ask what the budget for the position is. If you must quote a salary figure, state a range, i.e., between $4.50 and $6.00 an hour, or $600 to $1,000 a month, or $12,000 to $15,000 a year. Before giving a salary quote be sure to do your homework. Find out what industry is paying for this type of position.

An interviewer may NOT ask you questions which are not job related. These include questions which focus on your age, social group, religious or political preferences, background, national origin, or sex. Questions about marital status, dependents, and family plans are also inappropriate. Each person needs to decide whether or not he/she wishes to respond to any of these questions if they are brought up at the interview. You may choose to politely refuse to answer these questions or you could inquire how this information fits in with the job, i.e., if asked about dependents you could ask if the company provides a day care center.

"YES, YOU COULD SAY I HAVE ARROW-DYNAMIC EXPERIENCE. WHY DO YOU ASK?"

DRIVING LESSONS

1. Be at least ten minutes early for your appointment. Allow up to two hours for each interview.

2. Do not bring anyone with you.

3. Body language: Walk in confidently. Shake your interviewer's hand firmly. Assume an "open" position: arms at side, feet firmly on the floor, thrust your body slightly forward, and keep your head up. Keep your hands inactive; don't fiddle. Look the interviewer in the eye, especially when answering questions.

4. Do not chew gum or smoke during the interview.

5. Listen attentively.

6. Avoid negative replies; leave personal problems at home.

7. Find out when a decision will be made and how you will be notified. This will help you to schedule your follow-up.

8. Tell the interviewer you want the job.

9. Send a follow-up letter. The follow-up letter is a courteous response to an interviewer and should be treated as a routine part of the job search. It is your thank you to the interviewer for the interview. It should also restate your relevant qualifications and desire for the job. Follow the same mechanical set-up used for the cover letter.

What they always want to know and aren't afraid to ask

COMMON INTERVIEW QUESTIONS USED BY EMPLOYERS

In order to practice answering questions write down your answers on a separate piece of paper, or have someone ask you these questions orally.

1. What are your long range and short range goals? When and why did you establish these goals? How are you preparing to achieve them?

2. What do you see yourself doing five years from now? What do you expect to be earning at that time?

3. What do you really want to do in life?

4. How do you plan to achieve your career goals?

5. Which is more important to you the money or the job? What are the most important rewards you expect to receive from your career?

6. Why do you want to be a_____?

7. What do you consider your **greatest** strengths and weaknesses as an employee?

8. What motivates you to put forth your **greatest** effort?

9. How has your education and training prepared you for your career?

10. WHY SHOULD I HIRE YOU?

11. What do you think it takes to become successful?

12. What qualities should a successful manager possess?

13. Do you have plans for continued education?

14. In your past training what courses did you like best? least? Why?

15. What courses did you do best in? Do you think your grades are a good indication of your academic achievement and abilities?

16. How would you describe the ideal job for you? In what kind of work environment are you most comfortable?

17. Do you work well under pressure?

18. What do you know about our company? Why did you apply here?

19. Are you willing to spend at least 6 months as a trainee?

20. What types of people appeal most/least as coworkers? Do you prefer working with others or by yourself?

21. What did you like most about your last job? least? How did previous employers treat you?

22. What have you done that shows initiative and willingness to work?

23. What salary do you expect?

24. How many days were you absent from school? work?

25. What hours do you prefer working? When can you start?

JUST AS SOMEONE IS INTERVIEWING YOU FOR YOUR QUALIFICATIONS, YOU ARE LOOKING TO SEE IF THE JOB IS RIGHT FOR YOU.

CHECK OUT THE TERRAIN

SAMPLE QUESTIONS THAT YOU CAN ASK THE COMPANY . . .

1. Would you mind describing the duties of the job?

2. What abilities do you need most in people on this job?

3. Could you tell me about the people I'd be working with?

4. What happened to the last person who had this job? If the person was fired ask why.

5. What is your promotional policy?

6. Do you have tuition refund or reimbursement for additional training taken outside the company? Is there any in-house training?

7. In general terms, what are the company's growth projections?

AFTER YOU HAVE BEEN OFFERED A JOB OR AFTER THE COMPANY HAS SHOWN STRONG INTEREST, YOU MAY ASK . . .

1. What is the salary of this job?

2. What is the salary review policy and how regularly will this be done?

3. What is the benefit package?

4. Could I have a tour of the work site?

5. Who will be my supervisor? May I meet this person?

6. Could I talk with someone who is doing the same job?

ALIGN AND BALANCE

SELF-EVALUATION POST INTERVIEW RATING

To assess your interview strengths and weaknesses after each interview rate your performance according to the following questions on a scale of 1 to 10, with 10 being the highest rating.

1. Did I look as good as I'm capable of looking?

2. Was I as informed about the company as I should have been?

3. Was I relaxed and in control of myself?

4. Did I answer the questions in a way that stressed the three most important things: my **ability,** my **willingness,** and my **suitability** to do the job?

5. Did I **listen** to the interviewer?

6. Did I steer questions toward the points I wanted to stress?

7. Was I observant enough?

8. Did the interviewer get interested and involved in what I was saying?

9. Did I tailor my answers to the type of interviewer who interviewed me?

10. Did I present an accurate and favorable picture of myself?

ADDITIONAL COMMENTS:

CHOOSING THE RIGHT HIGHWAY

DECIDING ON A JOB OFFER

Eventually a decision must be made on whether or not to accept a job offer. Such a decison may appear overwhelming. Compare the job with personal needs and balance it against potential job offers. This decision should not be taken lightly. Take the time needed. Remember, this decision will dramatically affect lifestyle and future career options.

Requesting time to decide from an employer can be a difficult, but not impossible, task. Some employers will want an immediate answer, but most will be willing to give you a few days to think about it if you ask. Be positive about the employer's job offer when asking for time to decide. If you still have some unanswered questions about the company or the job, now is the time to ask for an appointment to go over these questions.

Since an employer will not wait more than a week for your decision, you have to get competitive offers quickly. This requires immediate follow-up with previously contacted employers.

One final word about decision making: DON'T PANIC. Consider all the options before making a choice. Don't be pushed into a bad decision. In other words, do not grab an offer until you are satisfied that it is a good job for you.

ARRIVAL

You have found the job meant for you. Now you want to make sure you succeed. It is worth noting that 90% of the workers who fail do so because of an attitude problem. Here are a few pointers that will help you become successful in your new job.

CITY ORDINANCES

STAY TUNED

1. It's your responsibility to get along with the boss, not the other way around. No one gives you happiness, you create it for yourself. Staying happy on the job is your responsibility.

USE SCANNER

2. In a new job it's important to watch and listen for a long time to discover the unwritten rules and expectations.

RIGHT TURN ON RED

3. Learn to ask for help. Don't hesitate to ask your boss or co-workers any questions you may have about your job.

YIELD

4. Accept criticism gracefully. Everyone makes mistakes and so will you. Learn by your mistakes and concentrate on not repeating them.

NO FREE PARKING

5. On every job there are some disagreeable tasks; accept your share without complaint.

BE A GOOD SAMARITAN

6. Be considerate of your co-workers. When you are not busy, offer to help someone who is.

USE ALL YOUR HORSEPOWER

7. Strive for improvement in the performance of your job. Work hard and do the best job of which you are capable.

ALLOW FOR HEAVY TRAFFIC

8. Always be on time to work; know how long it takes to get there. Be absent only when absolutely necessary.

DON'T HOG THE AIRWAYS

9. Limit personal phone calls.

HIT THE BRAKES

10. Your personal problems are just that. Keep them to yourself.

Appendix A : Resume Examples

TERRI MCDONOUGH
2947 Penrose Ave
Philadelphia, PA 91945
Phone: 568-7881

OBJECTIVE: Seeking a position as a <u>General Office Clerk</u> where ability to follow directions and meet deadlines in a cheerful manner would be desirable.

EDUCATION:

Philadelphia Technological Center	Franklin School
593 Manning Walk	45 Haws Lane
Philadelphia, PA 19106	Philadelphia, PA 19118
Attended: June 1983-March 1984	Attended: Sep. 1977-June 1980
Course: <u>General Office Practice</u>	Course: <u>General Academic</u>
Diploma: Excellent Attendance	Diploma: Excellent Attendance

TECHNICAL JOB SKILLS:

10 Key Calculator	Typewriter	General Office Skills
Apple II Computer,	Filing	Data Processor
CRT (Cathode Ray Tube)	Record Keeping	

JOB HISTORY:

Present Employer: Mardsen Maintenance Co.
                                317 Balfour St. Philadelphia, PA 19134
                                Supervisor: Tom Hollenbeck (783-9023)
Job Description: Custodian

Former Employer: K-Mart
                                191 Farragut Ave. S., Philadelphia, PA 19139
                                Supervisor: Richard Moore
Job Description: Cashier

Former Employer: Sears
   1980   Uptown Mall
                                  Supervisor: Pamela Bottolffln (no phone)
Job Description: Operated Specialty Jewelry Stand

CHARACTER ASSESSMENT:

I consider myself to be an industrious, punctual, hardworking and conscientious employee. I can relate well to others and I feel I'd be an asset to any firm.

My educational plans include attending night school on a part-time basis, taking classes in Data Processing.

References and Transcripts Available on Request

John R. Jones
2135 Skyway Drive
Chicago, IL 69023
(312) 790-5562

CAREER OBJECTIVE

To obtain a position in traffic transportation which will utilize acquired organizing
and communication skills. Desire to advance to administrative or managerial status.

PROFESSIONAL TRAINING

1983-1984   Chicago Institute of Technology
                   Freight Transportation Management
                   G.P.A.-3.50

1979-1980   American Technical Society
                   Practical Business Administration
                   G.P.A.-3.50

TECHNICAL SKILLS

Warehouse Operation   Rate analysis
Auditing Freight Bills   City Dispatch
Inventory Controls   Accounting Procedures
Tracing (O.S. & I.)   Data Processing
Tariff Interpretation   Typing (40 wpm)

EMPLOYMENT HISTORY

1980-1984   Property Manager
          Northern Properties Corporation; Chicago, Illinois
          Manager, multiple unit housing complexes

1976-1980   Driver/Dockman
          Century-Mercury Motor Freight; Chicago, Illinois
          Loaded and unloaded freight, maintained shipment records.

1974-1976   Customer Service
          Chicago Union Depot; Chicago, Illinois
          Provided passenger services: sold tickets, made reservations, handled
          claims and complaints.

1973-1974   Delivery
          Package Delivery Service; Decatur, Illinois

CHARACTER SUMMARY

Highly motivated individual who approaches each task as a learning experience.
Possess detail and perfrection oriented work habits. Stable background: happily
married, 2 children. Non Smoker (excellent health).

References and Transcripts Available on Request

ANN THOMPSON
356 E Marie #308
W. St. Paul, MN 55118
Residence: 457-6036

OBJECTIVE

To obtain a position in a progressive salon which keeps current with new trends.
Have strong desire to perfect technical skills and develop a loyal following.

EDUCATION

St. Paul TVI   Major: Cosmetology
235 Marshall Avenue   Grade Point Average A
St. Paul, MN 55102

Inver Hills Community College   Curriculum Included:
8445 E. College Trail   Human Service courses
Inver Grove Heights, MN 55075   Small Business Management

SALON SERVICE EXPERIENCE

PRACTICAL   CHEMICAL   THEORY
Hairstyling   Permanent Waves   Redken System
Hairshaping   Reverse Perms   Trichology
Manicures/Pedicures   Relaxers   Chemistry
Sculptured Nails   Colors   Trichoanalysis
Make-up/Skin Care

EMPLOYMENT

May 1983 to Present   August 1980 to December 1982
MGM Liquor Warehouse   Sun Newspapers
1690 S. Robert Street   7401 Bush Lake Road
West St. Paul, MN 55118   Edina, MN 55435
Phone: 455-4474   Phone: 831-1200
CASHIER   CREDIT COLLECTOR

April 1982 to May 1983
Ground Round
1500 E. 78th Street
Richfield, MN 55420
Phone: 866-4911
HOSTESS

ACHIEVEMENTS

Member of the National Hairdressers Association.
Certified in Trichoanalysis.
Energetic, Enthusiastic and Self Motivated Cosmetologist.
Areas of Strength: Make-overs (Facials, Make-up Application and Haircutting).

Transcripts and References available on request.

LINDA RICE
14980 Canyon Road
Phoenix, Arizona 85020

OBJECTIVE
To obtain unit coordinator/unit clerk position in health care
facility.

EDUCATION

Hanlon Technical College
4900 W. 5th Street
Phoenix, Az. 85021

Graduated: Health Unit Coordinator   August 1984
            Nursing Assistant   March 1981

EMPLOYMENT
Hinkley Manufacturing   Clerk
Phoenix, Az 85021   8-1979 to 11-1980

Greeley Health Care   Nursing Assistant
Phoenix, Az 85020   4-1981 to present

SKILLS

Clerical
Assumed total coordination of business payroll for
    50 employees
Maintained records of company sales
Coordinated accounts receivable
Created and implemented inventory control procedures

Communications
Exercised public relations skills
Utilized telecommunication skills
Responded to customer needs and complaints

Health Care
Set priorities in meeting patient needs
Worked cooperatively on nursing team
Responded calmly in emergency situations
Exercised flexibility in working on several units

Volunteer Experience
1976-1979   Hospital Volunteer: Assisted hospital
                employees and visited patients
1980 to present Johnson Elementary: "Bucket Brigade":
                Taught learning disabled children on
                one-to-one basis.
PRIMARY ASSETS
Friendly, outgoing personality
Excellent attendance
Maintain composure in stressful situations
Dependable, able to work independently
Reliable and conscientious

References available upon request.

STEVEN JOHN LISKA
2160 Timmy Street
Mascabarqua, NJ 89436
(213) 560-3485

OBJECTIVE: Pipefitter-Steamfitter

SUMMARY OF EXPERIENCE:

- Pipefitting
- Drawing and Blueprint Reading   • Welding
- Air Conditioning   • Electricity
- Heating (hot water and steam)   • Refrigeration

WORK RECORD:

2/84-Present   Roadway Custom Trailors
                        3248 Terminal Drive
                        Fabrication Welder, Painter

6/82-Present   Self-employed
                        Landscaper; billing estimating

6/80-Present   Daly-Kampmeyer Properties
                        Grand Properties
                        600 Northern Federal Building
                        Carpenter; Remodel houses

6/78-Present   Kurth Construction Inc.
                        1096 Cullen Avenue
                        Landscape Maintenance Design; Carpenter; Roofer

6/79-9/80   Kraus-Anderson Construction Co.
                        525 South Eighth Street
                        Cement worker; operated jackhammer, power buggy

EDUCATION:

                        Bakersfield School of Mechanical Engineering
                        Pipefitting Program. Graduate 1984.

ACHIEVEMENTS: (Awards)

- President of Vocational Industrial Clubs of America at Bakersfield School
  of Mechanical Engineering
- President of GOFA (Give Once for All) charity organization
- VICA State Officer Candidate
- Certified in Cardiopulmonary Resuscitation and Advanced First Aid
- Certified Commercial Diver; wreck and cavern diver
- Participated in Ironman 100; Bicycle Tour '83

REFERENCES AVAILABLE ON REQUEST

MARIA GARCIA
1300 Ocean View Lane
Pacific Palisades, California 94302
Residence: 995-4356

OBJECTIVE

To secure a position in a medical facility where training as a medical secretary can be applied.

EDUCATION

Santa Monica Junior College   Medical Secretary
Santa Monica, California 90403   A. A. Degree 1985

Core courses: Three quarters of medical terminology including anatomy and physiology, medical typing, and medical transcription. Also, medical health care law, business English, interpersonal communication, and general psychology.

West High School   Diploma 1981
Pacific Palisades, California 90272

Activities: Year book business staff, canteen council, student council, treasurer local chapter OEA.

SKILLS

• Type accurately 60 wpm   • Word Processing:
• 13 months CRT   — IBM Displaywriter
• Good spelling   — WANG
• Medical Recordkeeping   — AB-Dick

EMPLOYMENT

Beverly Hills Hotel   1981 to present
Los Angeles, California 90025

Responsibilities: Front desk, Reservations, Cashier

Gained an understanding of working with people directly as well as through telephone correspondence. Learned to work independently and set priorities to efficiently complete work.

PERSONAL ASSESSMENT

Strive for perfection and consider myself to be a dedicated worker. Capable of following instructions and meeting deadlines while producing accurate work.

References furnished on request.

Peter Biever
1423 E. 46th St.
Washington, D.C.
Residence: 696-6122

POSITION OBJECTIVE

Auto Mechanic: Trained to use computer controlled diagnostic equipment
and capable of performing all repairs expected of a full service mechanic.

QUALIFICATION SUMMARY

Successfully completed two years of auto mechanic training and one year of
specialized training in Computered Controlled Fuel and Ignition Systems.
Able to diagnose and repair all current computerized cars. Trained and
experienced in all other aspects of the auto mechanic field. Proficient at
the use of all related machinery as well as power and air tools.

TRADE EDUCATION

Washington D.C. Area Technical Vocational Institute
1658 Collins Ave.
Washington, D.C.
Graduate: Automotive Diagnostic Technician

Smythe Trades and Industries Center
432 23rd Ave. S.
Washington, D.C.
Graduate: Auto Mechanics

TECHNICAL BACKGROUND

Trained in all aspects of the automotive repair field. Specialized in
computer controlled fuel and ignition systems. Experienced in: Brakes,
Tune-up, Electrical Troubleshooting, Transmissions (automatic and
standard), Major Engine Repair, Front End Alignment and Suspensions, and
Air Conditioning.

TRADE RELATED EMPLOYMENT

Lloyd's Automotive Service   1/84 Present
Washington, D.C.   Gas Attendant/ Light Mechanical

Precision Tune   6/83-9/83
Washington, D.C.   Mechanic

John's One Stop Car Shop   10/81-1/82
Washington, D.C.   Gas Attendant/Light Mechanical

References Furnished Upon Request.

THERESA LOWEN
5583 Winslow Ave.
Newark, NJ 45720
(314) 235-8924

OBJECTIVE

To obtain a position as a clerk typist. Offer typing speed of 50 WPM, and the ability to work independently.

EDUCATION

New Jersey School of Business
1784-7th St.
Hampdten, NJ 34729

GRADUATED: General Office Practice

ACQUIRED SKILLS

Received practical experience in beginning typing, including the production of letters, manuscripts and basic office correspondence. Developed skills in the operations of various calculating machines. During Model Office, practiced performing simulated office tasks which included typing, calculating prices, inventory, payroll billing, record keeping, and computer usage. Received hands on experience on a CRT.

EMPLOYMENT

All Nations Insurance	American Hoist
534 East Rangoon	3903 Westphalia
Newark, NJ 45823	Newark, NJ 45901
Claims Clerk	File Clerk
1/80 to 5/80	8/78 to 12/78

Zayre's
Robin Street N
North Newark, NJ 45317

Cashier
5/77 to 12/77

PERSONAL ATTRIBUTES

Maintained a "B" average throughout training. Neat, orderly, and efficient worker; able to work with others.

Hardworker   Dependable   Self Confident   Cooperative

References Available on Request

Shelly M. Crotty
558 Concord St.
Tulsa, OK 24943
Home phone: (819) 776-2215

OBJECTIVE

To obtain employment in the Graphic Arts field that will utilize my talents and education. Areas of specialization:

Silkscreening: •custom T-shirts   •acrylic clocks

Layout & Design: •two color overlays   •assemb. photographic type

Camera-Darkroom: •contacting, linework   •halftones, duotones

EDUCATION

Tulsa Vocational Technical Institute   Majored in Graphic Arts
1479 Oakland Pkwy.   Graduate
Tulsa, OK 24784

Rolland Senior High   General Study
367 E. Eder St.   Graphic Arts (3 yrs.)
Tulsa, OK 24785   Graduate

EMPLOYMENT

Arthur Salm, Inc.   Cabinet Supply Co.
1156 Industrial Blvd.   6000 Brunson Ave.
Tulsa, OK 24578   Tulsa, OK 24579
From 9/82 - 2/83   Summers of 1979 to 1982
Silkscreener   Residential Construction
Duties: Silkscreened, prepared screens   Duties: Light construction,
for darkroom, opaqued screens.   use of power and hand tools,
                                              some painting, sheetrocking,
                                              and tile work.

ACHIEVEMENTS

*Design and produce glass etchings, which I sell commercially.

*Successfully completed 15 month training in Graphic Arts; Held a B Average.

*Have done volunteer work at Community Health Clinic, including poster-work, fund raising, ticket selling.

*Enjoy most competitive sports; played basketball, softball, and was manager for volleyball team in high school.

References furnished on request.

Marilyn James
62 Haught St.
Indianapolis, IN 34204
Phone: (317) 857-4114

POSITION OBJECTIVE: Cost Accountant, Materials Management Coordinator

BUSINESS TRAINING: Weldon W. Wright Vo-Tech
                        500 E. Summit Parkway.
1982-1984   Indianapolis, Indiana

                        Major: Accounting

                        Oliver Business School
                        7850 Gem St.
1975-1976   Gary, Indiana

                        Major: Business Administration

WORK EXPERIENCE: Cost Accounting Clerk   Heritage, Inc.

1981-1983   Individually priced all items for customer orders. All job
                        information was initiated and maintained from
                        salesman's order to customer billing.

1980-1981   Inventory Coordinator   Cole-Sewell

                        Developed and coordinated the Inventory Control
                        Department. The perpetual inventory developed kept
                        records as correct as possible. My knowledge of
                        material Requirements Planning enabled me to devise
                        this system.

PERSONAL REMARKS: Take pride in organizing and systems development
                        abilities. The pressure of deadlines brings out my best
                        performance.

                References and Transcripts Available on Request

Miriam Jacobs-Cohen

•1255 East Sixth Street   •Portland, Oregon 92707   •(503) 455-6366

POSITION OBJECTIVE: **LEGAL SECRETARY**

LEGAL WORK EXPERIENCE

    1982 to 1985
    Benjamin, Knowles, and Wolfe
    301 Federal Building
    Portland, Oregon 92707

    Legal Secretary-typing of correspondence pertaining to real estate
    transaction and corporate law. Took dictation from three attorneys.
    Responsible for billing. Set-up and maintained files.

    1980 to 1981
    Seeny, Todd, and Rabinowitz.
    First National Bank Building
    Suite 223
    Portland, Oregon 92707

    Receptionist-greeted clients, scheduled and coordinated appointment
    calendars, answered phones and connected calls.

EDUCATIONAL BACKGROUND

    Legal Secretarial Program   Course work:
    Portland Technical Institute   legal typing (80 wpm)
    500 Industrial Boulevard   legal office procedures
    Portland, Oregon 92722   legal transcription (90)
                                         business law
    1985 graduate   legal terminology
    GPA 3.75   accounting

    Fashion Merchandising/modeling   Course work:
    Lowthian Fashion School   business and marketing
    3500 Lemon Lane   human relations
    Portland, Oregon 92730   management and supervision
                                         women in business
    1982 Graduate   modeling
    GPA 3.9

PERSONAL REMARKS

    Take pride in producing correspondence quickly and efficiently. The
    pressure of deadlines brings out my best performance. Enjoy exercising
    organizational abilities.

            REFERENCES AND TRANSCRIPTS WILL BE SUBMITTED ON REQUEST

TYRONE JONES
45 South Parkway #10   Home phone: (312) 558-2340
Chicago, IL 60621

OBJECTIVE   Position as a computer programmer/analyst with a firm that
                   will use my systems, programming, and operations knowledge
                   fully.

EDUCATION   South Chicago Community College   1985
                   2000 Madison Avenue   A. A. Degree
                   Chicago, IL 60616

                   22 month course in Computer Programming earning 135 credits

                   Woolwich Polytechnic School for boys
                   Macbaen Street
                   Woolwich, London W.E. 18, U. K.
                                                               1979
                   Honors student   High School Diploma

WORK EXPERIENCE   Economics Laboratory   PRODUCTION CONTROL ANALYST

6/83 - 3/85   Responsible for maintaining daily production schedule of
                   business applications systems. Communicate with operators,
  2700 hours   programmers, analysts, data entry, and users as necessary,
                   identifying, reviewing, resolving and documenting problems
                   with production jobs and parallel testing. Analyze user's
                   needs and try to maintain high service level. Light batch
                   programming in COBOL, EAZYTREV, CA/SORT, and VSAM.

                   South Chicago Public Schools   EDUCATIONAL ASSISTANT

4/84 - 6/85   Responsible for operating system, consoles and associated
                   peripherals. Helped students debug programs and JCL,
  1300 hours   showing them how to log on to and use the system. Backed
                   up files as required.

ACTIVITIES   . Vice president local chapter OEA

                   . Student representative

                   . Placed third in state competition for computer programming

---

REFERENCES   Delivered on request

Sally Kaysen
8735 Lanewood Ave.
Houston, TX 77016
(563-8910)

POSITION OBJECTIVE: To obtain position in a salon which offers
opportunities for personal advancement and keeps
current with the new trends.

TECHNICAL EDUCATION: Houston School of Cosmetology
675 Durness Way
Houston, TX 77025

The 1500 hours of training included two quarters of
theory and two quarters of clinical floor.

EMPLOYMENT: Texas Childrens Hospital
10/80-5/81   6621 Fannin St. Houston, TX 77030
Position: Receptionist

9/78-6/80   Bridgemans Restaurant
591 Ascalon Cir. Houston, TX 77069
Position: Waitress

PERSONAL STATEMENT: Desire and ability to work with public led to
pursuing training in the field of cosmetology.
Maintained straight A average throughout
training. Held an excellent attendance record.

EXPERIENCED IN: · Haircutting   · Scalp treatments
· Permanent waving   · Manicures
· Hair coloring   · Facials
· Shampoo and sets   · Fingerwaves

References available upon request

DONALD J. MAZZALLE
1000 Edgerton #1390
Tampa, FL 89341
Home Phone (901) 783-8912

OBJECTIVE:	To secure a positon as a line mechanic where desire to expand skills gained in technical training is encouraged.
TRADE EDUCATION:	Orlando School of Vocational Training 34782-28th St. Orlando, FL 89782 Major Area: Industrial Hydraulics and Pneumatics Graduated 1983
RELATED TRAINING:	Hyraulics and Pneumatic Logic, Blue Print Reading, Machine Shop, Basic Electricity, Basic Electrical Controls, and Welding.
MILITARY:	1974 to 1976 United States Army Truck Driver Award: 25,000 accident free miles. Honorable Discharge
WORK HISTORY:	
1982-1983	American Building Maintenance, Orlando, FL 68912 Janitor Established a routine to get things done on time in an orderly way.
1981-1982	Diamond Cab Company, Orlando, FL 69802 Cab Driver Worked on a commission; learned motivation and acquired the ability to get along well with people.
1979-1981	Union Gospel Mission , Orlando, FL 69852 and Columbia Transit, Orlando, FL 67441 Bus and Truck Driver Developed people management skills.
1978-1979	Gross and Given Manufacturing, Tampa, FL 68941 Shear Operator Helper Perfected ability to produce precision work and established good work habits.
PERSONAL REMARKS:	Capable of solving problems in a careful, orderly and efficient manner. Function well under stress and can meet deadlines.

TRANSCRIPTS AND REFERENCES AVAILABLE ON REQUEST.

Cindy Simpson
5000 Meadowbrook Lane
Kansas City, Kansas 66117
(913) 834-9854

CAREER OBJECTIVE

Seeking a position in transportation, directed toward traffic management.

TECHNICAL EDUCATION

1983-1985   Kansas City Vo-Tech
FREIGHT TRANSPORTATION AND TRAFFIC MANAGEMENT

   *strong emphasis on freight transportation and on ICC and DOT
    regulations

   *Secretary, Delta Nu Alpha (transportation fraternity)

Traffic skills include: - Freightrate calculations   - OS&D claims
                        - Tariff interpretations   - Traffic management
                        - Warehouse operations   - Business correspondence

Complementary courses: Accounting (2), Business law, Typing (2), business
                       communications, Data processing, Human Relations,
                       Supervision.

CAREER RELATED WORK EXPERIENCE

1983 to 1984   E. L. MURPHY

Revenue Clerk; computed and prepared revenue reports. Worked closely with the
company's computer programmer and with the marketing and sales departments.

1982   AMERICAN TRUCK DISPATCH

Broker; first introduction to the transportation field. Became intrigued by
the fast moving transportation industry.

SPECIAL SKILLS

•typing (50 wpm)   •filing   •microcomponent soldering   •10 key adding

CHARACTER ASSESSMENT

Hardworking and well organized; able to work at a professional pace. Self
motivated and goal oriented; strive to produce quality work.

ELIZABETH H. BERAN
616 E 15th St., #506
Keldron, SD 57634

OBJECTIVE

To develop a career which utilizes skills as Medical Laboratory
Technician as well as interpersonal communication abilities.

EDUCATION

Mobridge Technical Institute (TI)
Mobridge, SD

Associate Degree:
Medical Laboratory Technology
GPA: 3.85

University of South Dakota
Brookings, SD

Bachelor of Arts Degree:
Studio Art
GPA: 3.5

ACCREDITATION

·American Society of Clinical Pathologists
·National Certification Agency

CLINICAL

·Hematology and Coagulation
·Chemistry
·Urinalysis
·Immunohematology

·Microbiology
·Mycology
·Parasitology
·Immunology

Received six months training.

EMPLOYMENT

Mobridge TI
Mobridge, SD
Lab Aide/Tutor
1983-1984

Renaissance Festival
Denver, CO
Safety Services
(First Aid, CPR, Security)
1983-1984 Seasons

Annie's Parlour
Brookings, SD
Waitress
1981-present

ASSOCIATION

·American Society for Medical Technologists

ACTIVITIES

Participated in three cultural exchanges:
    ·Greece - 2 months - Youth For Understanding
    ·Mexico - 3 months - Study of Arts and Language
    ·Europe - 2 months - Extensive Travel

Speak conversational Spanish and German.

References and additional employment record available upon request.

ANGELA M. CAPKO
Apartment 4
3101-12th Avenue South
Aspen, CO 67234
(451) 356-7879

OBJECTIVE

To work as a full-time office bookkeeper which will utilize office knowledge and skills; eager to perform day-by-day tasks within a company.

EDUCATION

Colorado Business College
1453-76th St.
Aspen, CO 67423

Major: Bookkeeping/Clerical
Graduated March 1984

Roslyn Park Senior High School
310 Gernad St.
Aspen, CO 67528

Major: Accounting I & II
Graduated June 1983

SKILLS

Completed 6 months training which covered all materials used in an office

- Journalizing
- Accounts Receivable
- Accounts Payable
- Sales

- Purchases
- Payroll
- Taxes
- Posting

- Statements
- Filing
- Typing

Equipment: IBM Selectric II typewriter, Apple II Computer, ten key

EMPLOYMENT EXPERIENCE

McDonalds
4121 Hiawatha Avenue
Aspen, CO 67529
(415) 672-6734
10/81-6/82
Customer Service

McDonalds
445 Indus Ave.
Aspen, CO 67528
(415) 892-8924
9/80-10/81
Customer Service

PERSONAL STATEMENT

Possess ability and strong desire to work with numbers and figures.
Honest, loyal, and trustworthy person.
Active member of (COEA) Colorado Office Education Association
Desire to increase business skills and knowledge.
Interested in advancement.

References available on request

KIET Q. HUYNH
83457 31st Ave. SE
New York, NY 34958
(387) 292-1663

OBJECTIVE

To obtain employment as graphic artist where knowledge of a variety of skills is desirable.

CAPABILITIES

Camera-Darkroom . . . . . Contacting, Line Work . . . . . Halftones, Duotones
Presses-A B Dick 36 . . . . Production Printing . . . . Four Color Runs
Platemaking . . . . Stripping Negatives . . . . Litho Platemaking

EDUCATION

Mason Avenue Technical Center
1478 Mason Avenue
New York, NY 34958

Major: Graphic Arts
Graduate
(1982-1984)

EMPLOYMENT

Pro A M Company
7819 31st St. NE Suite 11
New York, NY 34957

From: 12/81-6/82
Position: Janitor
Duties: Vacuum, floors, Bathrooms

The Wokery Restaurant
1411 South Actan Ave.
Queens, NY 39857

From: 4/83-5/84
Position: Cook Helper
Duties: Prepare
foods for cooking

ACHIEVEMENTS

-Successfully completed 15 months training in Graphic Arts.

-Maintained a "B" average throughout Graphic Arts training.

-Work well with others. Creative, hard worker and well-organized.

-Enjoy most competitive sports, movies and traveling.

REFERENCES

References and transcripts available upon request.

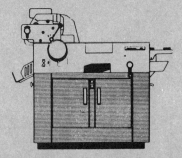

Gayle E. Teigen
362 Jenks Avenue
St. Paul, MN 55101
Telephone: (612) 771-7658

Objective

Short Range:

    To establish a responsible working position in Graphic Arts that will
utilize skills, knowledge, and abilities in press operations.

Long Range:

    To extend my abilities into Graphic Sales.

Qualifications

Hours:

420   Letterpress, Duplicator, and Flexographic Presses.
       (Davidson 500, A.B. Dick 360, Itek, Chief 17, Multilith-1250-
       1250W, Heidelberg Ltr. press, and Hamada offset.

420   Large Litho Presses, Bindery and Silk Screening Techniques.

       Includes pressroom safety, pressroom housekeeping, principles
       of machinery, care and maintenance of ink systems, dampening
       systems, handling paper in the pressroom, care and loading
       of feeders, binding operations, princples of bindery machines
       and practice in production printing.

240   Stripping/Platemaking.

       Includes layout practice, stripping procedures, line and half-
       tone, photographic negatives, inspection and proofing, care
       of flats, litho platemaking, use of chemicals and measurements
       in platemaking.

240   Camera-Darkroom and Pastemakeup.

       Includes assembling of photographic type, borders, designs
       and reproduction proofs into complete pages in one or more
       colors by means of overlays. Also involves mixing chemicals,
       contacting, line work, reductions and blow-ups, halftones
       and duotones.

240   Computer assisted Phototypesetting and Composing.

       Includes composition, the process of setting and arranging
       type by the use of hand set type or computer assisted
       phototypesetting.

Education

St. Paul Technical Vocational Institute
235 Marshall Ave.
St. Paul, MN 55102

Graphic Arts
Graduated 1984
Grade Pt. Average: B

St. Paul Adult Ed. Center
Marshall & Ivy
St. Paul, MN 55104

General Ed. Diploma
Graduated 1977

Employment

Quality Park Product
2520 Como Ave.
St. Paul, MN 55104
Press Operator-1980

Twin City Tool & Die
1070 33 Ave. S.E.
Mpls., MN 55104
Punch Press Operator
1978-1979

J.D. Products
780 Kasota Ave.
Mpls., MN 55104
Plastic Injection Mold
Press Operator 1975-77

Personal Statement

Hard working and eager to apply training to a fast-paced, progressive working environment with a successful company. Mechancial aptitude and experience has led me to further my knowledge in press operations.

References

Excellent personal references and vocational transcripts available upon request.

Appendix B :

Cover letter Examples

430 Laurel Street
Austin, TX 78710
October 13, 1983

Mr. John Jones
Personnel Supervisor
Custom Business Forms
10 Hennepin Avenue
Houston, TX 77201

Dear Mr. Jones:

   I am writing to you regarding the camera position you advertised in the paper.
I am seeking a position such as you described and am very interested in working
for your company.

   Having acquired thorough knowledge and training in the Graphic Arts field at
Houston T.V.I., I feel I am well suited and experienced for the job. I maintained a
"B" average in both shop and related courses at T.V.I. Enclosed is my resume
and a brochure for T.V.I. that will explain in greater detail the training I received.

   My strongest interest and talents were in camera work and stripping and
platemaking. In camera I have worked with black and white line work and
halftones/duotones. I received an A on all completed projects.

   I consider myself hard-working, attentive to my job, and willing to try new
things. I enjoy working with others and have had previous job experience dealing
with the public.

   I appreciate your consideration and I am looking forward to meeting you in a
personal interview. I will contact you next week to arrange a convenient interview
time and date.

                                        Sincerely yours,

                                        Penny Brown
                                        Penny Brown

Enclosure

2160 Timmy Street
Masquabarqua, NJ 89436
December 12, 1984

Mrs. Sharon Kutz
Acme Pipefitting, Incorporated
678 North Hampton Ave.
Center City, NJ 89453

Dear Mrs. Kutz:

I am interested in working with Acme Pipefitting Incorporated, on the new World
Trade Center in Center City, New Jersey. I would like to gain a challenging and
responsible position in pipefitting that will expand and utilize my training and
perfect technical skills. It is my understanding that your company needs a
pipefitter, so I want to tell you some of the things I can do.

I have worked in the construction trades for the past six years. From this
experience I have gained the ability to meet deadlines and to accurately perform
work meeting union standards. I am an organized, productive worker who enjoys
working with his hands as well as his mind.

Aside from my past work experience, I have completed a one-year program majoring
in pipefitting at Center City School of Trades and Industries. As a student there I
became involved in VICA, an organization that promotes leadership skills for
business and industry. For further information regarding my background and skills,
please review the enclosed resume.

I have confirmed our interview appointment on March 17, 1984, with your
secretary. I share the commitment to excellence for which Acme Pipefitting
Incorporated is noted. Thank you for your time and consideration. I am eagerly
looking forward to discussing employment possibilities with you.

Sincerely,

Steve Liska

Steve Liska

rh

Enclosure

312 West Butler Avenue
Boston, MA 02109
July 5, 1983

Elizabeth S. Wierum
Department 605
CRAY RESEARCH INC.
1440 Northland Drive
Boston, MA 02109

Dear Ms. Wierum:

I would be pleased to be considered for the position of Associate Graphic Specialist which was advertised in the paper. I feel that my strong interest, training, and educational background in graphic communications relates directly to your employment needs.

Along with my creative and technical skills, which are mentioned in my resume, are those skills of equal importance gained through my employment and personal experience. These are my ability to work hard and to work well with others, and my desire to maintain a positive and eager attitude.

A reasonable salary is important to me, but I am more interested in securing challenging employment and the opportunity to use and increase my skills. I am confident that I am capable of doing the quality of work for which your company is noted.

Thank you for your time and consideration. I am looking forward to meeting with you. I will contact you during the first part of the week to set up an interview appointment.

Sincerely,

Anne Volker

Anne Louise Volker

Enclosure

362 Jenks Avenue
St. Paul, MN 55101
October 12, 1983

Ms. Marcella Harfield
Cooperative Power Association
14615 Loan Oak Road
Eden Prairie, MN 55344

Dear Ms. Harfield:

Please accept my application for the position of Press Operator
which was advertised in the Sunday, October 9, 1983, edition
of the St. Paul Pioneer Press/Dispatch. I am enclosing a copy
of my resume for your review.

Pursuant to your ad, I have successfully completed the necessary
coursework at St. Paul Technical-Vocational Institute for Graphic
Arts. I am mechanically inclined, work well with my hands,
and take great pride in producing a quality finished product.
I feel I would be an asset to your organization and look forward
to the challenge a press operator's position with your firm
provides.

I would greatly appreciate the opportunity to be interviewed
for this particular position. I will be contacting you on
Monday to set up a specific interview time and date convenient
to us both.

Thank you in advance for your consideration.

                              Sincerely yours,

                              Gayle E. Teigen

                              Gayle E. Teigen

Enclosure

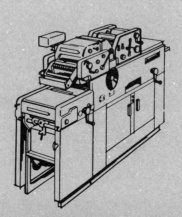

BETH PETROWSKE   7086 MILITARY ROAD   WOODBURY, MINNESOTA   55125

May 31, 1983

Mr. Jon Anderson
Colle McVoy Advertising Agency Inc.
1550 East 78th Street
Richfield, Minnesota 55423

Dear Mr. Anderson:

Yesterday I had the pleasure of touring your agency with my fellow
students at St. Paul Technical Vocational Institute. I was favorably
impressed and would be proud to be associated with a firm such as
Colle McVoy.

I am seeking a position as an Assistant Art Director or Copy Writer.
Given the chance, I feel my talents could be an asset to your company.

Training in both Commercial Art and Journalism has helped me gain good
communication skills, creative writing, and artistic abilities. I get
along well with people and have a strong desire to work and succeed
in the visual communications field. My qualifications are outlined
in the enclosed resume.

I would like to show you my portfolio and will be contacting you in a
few days to arrange an interview. Thank you for your time and
consideration.

Sincerely,

Beth A. Petrowske

Beth A. Petrowske

Enclosure

FABRIC SHOPPING

with

Alex Anderson

Seven Projects to Help You:

- Make Successful Choices

- Build Your Confidence

- Add to Your Fabric Stash

C&T PUBLISHING

© 2000 Alex Anderson

Illustrations and How-to Photography © 2000 C&T Publishing, Inc.

Developmental Editor: Liz Aneloski

Technical Editor: Joyce Engels Lytle

Copy Editor: Steve Cook

Design Direction: Diane Pedersen and Norman Remer

Front Cover and Book Design: Amante Quias

Back Cover Design: Kristen Yenche

Illustrator: Amante Quias

Quilt Photography: Sharon Risedorph

Cover Photo: John Bagley; taken at Going to Pieces, Pleasanton, California

Published by C&T Publishing, Inc., P.O. Box 1456, Lafayette, California 94549

Attention Teachers: C&T Publishing, Inc. encourages you to use this book as a text for teaching. Contact us at 800-284-1114 or www.ctpub.com for more information about the C&T Teachers Program.

Trademarked (™) and Registered Trademarked (®) names are used throughout this book. Rather than use the symbols with every occurrence of a trademark and registered trademark name, we are using the names only in an editorial fashion and to the benefit of the owner, with no intention of infringement.

We take great care to ensure that the information included in this book is accurate and presented in good faith, but no warranty is provided nor results guaranteed. Since we have no control over the choice of materials or procedures used, neither the author nor C&T Publishing, Inc. shall have any liability to any person or entity with respect to any loss or damage caused directly or indirectly by the information contained in this book.

Library of Congress Cataloging-in-Publication Data

Anderson, Alex

Fabric shopping with Alex Anderson : seven projects to help you make

successful choices, build your confidence, add to your fabric stash.

p. cm.

ISBN 1-57120-089-4 (paper trade)

1. Quilts--Design. 2. Patchwork--Equipment and supplies. 3. Textile

fabrics in art. 4. Color in textile crafts. I. Title.

TT835 .A51695 2000

746.46--dc21   99-050433

Printed in Singapore

10 9 8 7 6 5 4 3 2 1

Dedication

To all the quilting stores world-wide that supply us with beautiful fabrics and continually keep us inspired.

Acknowledgments

Being related to a possessed quilt-maker is not easy for my family at times; late dinners, endless phone conversations, and demanding schedules make our lives a little unpredictable. For their patience, understanding and sense of humor, I am most grateful.

I would especially like to thank Going to Pieces in Pleasanton, California, which graciously opened its doors to us to photo-graph the cover.

For their generosity, I would also like to thank:

Therm O Web, Inc. manufacturer of HeatnBond Iron-on Adhesives

Robert Kaufman Company

RJR Fashion Fabrics

P&B Textiles

Benartex Inc.

Cotton Patch

Contents

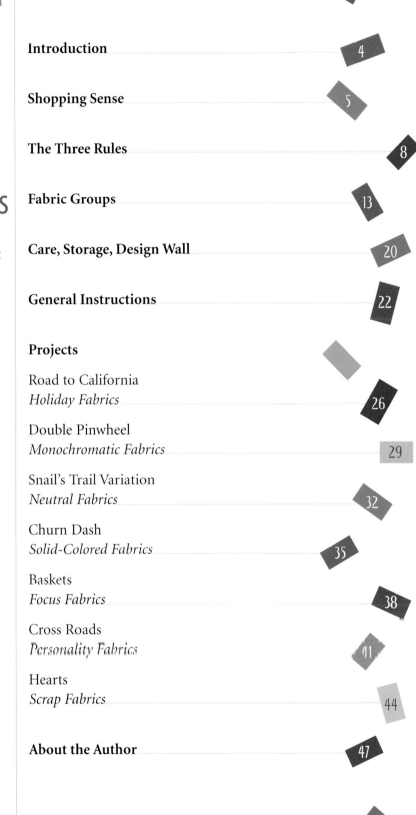

INTRODUCTION

I love fabric! The colors, patterns, and diversity of styles always inspire me. Nothing motivates me to start a new quilt more than a trip to the local quilt store. There's inspiration galore everywhere I look! However, for many people, even seasoned quiltmakers, shopping for fabric can be an overwhelming experience. I must confess that when I first started quilting, deciding which fabrics to buy wasn't easy. My brain would freeze and I would break out in a sweat when it was time to decide which fabrics to purchase. What if I made a mistake? Would I end up in Quilters' Jail? It took a little time to realize that all fabric purchased, used or unused, would end up in my stash, awaiting a future project—and that's good news.

One day in a class while attending San Francisco State University I decided to voice my strong personal likes and dislikes of certain colors. The teacher, Marika Contompasis, who could make color magic from a bag of ugly wool yarn, stopped the class and said, "To say you hate a color tells me you are ignorant of its use." I felt pretty embarrassed and have never looked at color the same since that day.

My mom puts it another way; to say you hate a color is like saying you hate a key on the piano—it's simply who it's played with. Your goal in quiltmaking should be to have the skills to look at any fabric and understand how to use it by knowing what other fabrics to use it with. Sure, there are still fabrics that aren't my favorites by themselves—and that's OK—but, believe it or not, those colors that I once condemned in that class are now at the top of my list of colors I use most. It was simply a matter of understanding how and when they should be used.

When it's time to start a quilt, two decisions need to be made at once: which quilt block to choose and what fabric group (pages 13–19) to use. I tend to use simpler quilt block patterns because I prefer to play with the fabric, not agonize over the block construction. I treat each block as an individual unit—using a different fabric combination. After a block is constructed it's time to move on to the next one. This method allows me the freedom to have fun experimenting with unusual fabrics and colors through the entire quiltmaking process. It doesn't really matter if a block ends up being too ugly to use, because not much time has been invested in the piecing process and, hopefully, something valuable has been learned. Does the block have dimension by the use of value? Is there a variety of size and scale of print? I analyze the pieced unit, learn from it, and move on. It is through the construction of each block that we learn which fabric combinations work and why.

It took several years of making painstaking decisions before I realized there were a few simple "Keys to Success" I could use for easily choosing and combining fabrics for my quilts. I will share many of my favorite fabric "Keys to Success," and explain how to work within each fabric group. Use them as guidelines. Before you know it, you will establish *your* own formulas that will give your quilts your special look!

This book is dedicated to teaching you how to become comfortable with fabric selection. You don't need to be a color genius to understand successful fabric combinations—it is simply a matter of understanding how to use different prints and colors in various combinations. So sit back, relax, enjoy, and be willing to take a few risks as you enter into the world of understanding fabrics and using them with confidence. I promise, it really is quite easy—and fun!

SHOPPING SENSE

Fortunately, there are several great quilt shops in the San Francisco Bay Area where I live. It is a little bit embarrassing, but I must confess that I get a rush every time I visit a quilt store.

Each shop has its own personality based on the owner's taste and buying style. The colors, prints, and arrangement of fabrics in these shops are an instant source of inspiration. The fabric collections create visual excitement, enticing me to buy.

How Fabrics are Organized in a Shop

When I first started quilting, a visit to the quilt shop was inspiring, but often overwhelming. I didn't know which way to turn or what direction to go. (It's kind of like clothes shopping with your teenage daughter!) You need to understand that each store has its own system of organizing the fabrics.

Within a few minutes of entering a quilt shop, it is important that you understand how the fabrics are organized, in order to make finding what you need an easier process. This will help you avoid feeling overwhelmed and makes the process of picking fabrics a joy, not a task.

The store closest to my home has three-tiered shelf units around the perimeter of the store. The fabric is organized by color family and is stacked from light to dark from the top shelf down. If I need a light blue, I know it will be on the top shelf. This system helps me target the fabric I need to look for. The newest collection of fabric is displayed on a shelf unit in the front of the store. Novelty, plaid, and batiks are each in their own sections. Upon first glance, a good quilt store can entice, inspire, and stimulate. Taking a few minutes to understand how the store is organized makes choosing fabrics a fun creative experience.

I love quilt stores and am never disappointed when visiting shops across the planet. In my opinion, fabric shopping is better than eating a hot fudge sundae on a warm summer day!

Deciding Which Fabrics You Need and How Much

To keep the fabric shopping experience from being overwhelming, I have a game plan for choosing fabrics. First I determine why I am purchasing fabric: for a new project; to keep my stash current; or simply that a piece of fabric is calling, begging me to take it home. This irresistible fabric has future plans that I am not aware of yet.

When it's time to start a new quilt, I visit the quilt store and purchase up to twenty pieces of new fabric. Then, when it's time to make the quilt, I integrate the new pieces into the quilt along with my support system of existing fabrics. This gives the quilt an updated look and also takes full advantage of my personal collection of fabric. For the projects in this book, I've given the total amount of yardage needed, but I can assure you that the greater the variety of fabrics you work with, the more exciting your quilt will be.

To keep my stash current and up-to-date, there are certain kinds of fabrics I am always seeking. The following fabric groups are main staples of every quilter's stash. Every time I go to the quilt store I look at the new fabrics that fall into the following categories and purchase the ones that will add something special to my collection.

I am frequently asked how much fabric to buy if I don't have a particular project in mind and am simply adding to my support system of fabric. The amount to purchase depends on the role the fabric is going to play, the size of your bank account, how much fabric storage space you have, and what type of fabric it is. Remember, the suggested amounts to purchase are simply my personal guidelines. As you become confortable with fabric shopping you will develop your own guidelines.

Tone-on-Tone Fabrics

Tone-on-tone fabrics are very subtle prints. They are monochromatic (one color) and often read as though they are solid-colored. These fabrics give the eyes a place to rest when used in a quilt. They add more interest and visual texture than solids and are forgiving if your piecing is not perfectly accurate. Typically I purchase ⅓ yard (¼ yard cuts get all tangled up in the washer and dryer like a shoestring).

Tone-on-Tone fabrics

Bridge Fabrics

A bridge fabric is a monochromatic print that has several color variations within one color family (page 10). These fabrics ease the transition of using many variations of one color family within a quilt. Notice how the fabric used on the top bar of each color family shown below pulls all the different colors within the one color family together. They are more difficult to find, so I purchase ½ yard.

Bridge fabrics

Sparkle Fabrics

Sparkle fabrics are monochromatic and have a complete range of value—light to dark (page 8). These fabrics are very lively and add a crisp look to quilts. They are fairly readily available, therefore ⅓ yard is an adequate amount to purchase.

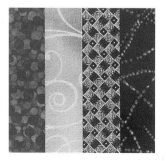

Sparkle fabrics

Polka Dot Fabrics

I love polka dots. They are fun and add a sense of whimsy to quilts. I think of polka dots as seasoning. A little goes a long way, but they make the quilt spicy. These fabrics are harder to find, so I usually buy ½ yard.

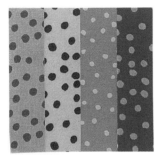

Polka Dot fabrics

Stripe Fabrics

Stripes add a sense of order to quilts. Sometimes a quilt gets visually overwhelming and the stripes help hold it all together. Stripes are especially good for inner borders. These fabrics are a little harder to find, therefore ¾ yard is a good amount to purchase.

Stripe fabrics

Focus Fabrics

Focus fabrics are large-scale prints with interesting color combinations. Two to three yards is a safe amount to have. This gives you enough if you decide to use it for the border. If not, it will work nicely for a pieced backing.

Focus fabrics

Novelty Fabrics

Novelty fabrics (also known as theme or conversational fabrics) have identifiable images printed on the fabric. A little novelty goes a long way; I usually buy ⅓ yard unless it is absolutely great, in which case I will buy a lot more, maybe up to 1 yard. It can always go on the back of a loved one's quilt.

Novelty fabrics

Conclusion

Because my quilts are so scrappy in nature, if I run out of a particular piece of fabric, there is no cause for distress. There will always be a new or better piece at the store to finish my quilt. I always welcome a trip to the quilt store, whether it is to purchase exciting new fabrics to mix with my existing stash to begin a new quilt, to buy special fabrics to add to my collection, or simply for inspiration to start a new quilt.

Fabric Quality

I try to work with the best 100%-cotton fabrics available from my local quilt store. These fabrics are the best available on the market. If you are bargain hunting somewhere other than your quilt store, it is extremely important to understand that the fabric might not be printed on first quality greige goods (the raw fabric the design is printed on). This may not seem important when you are first trying to establish your stash, but it can cause serious problems down the road. When the fabric is not top quality, all your hard work may be in vain. The quilt might fall apart right before your eyes or stretch and distort, making accurate piecing difficult. This disaster would be due to a lesser thread count (fewer threads per inch) and improper processing. In some classes I've taught, students have become quite frustrated because the bargain fabrics they brought in would not behave or piece together willingly. A lot of work goes into making a quilt, and your time is worth using the best products available. I would rather have five pieces of high quality fabric than twenty pieces of lesser quality.

THE THREE RULES

First and foremost, there are three rules that will help determine the success of your quilt: value, character of print, and color families. Please keep these in mind when choosing fabrics for your next quilt.

Value

Value is the degree of lightness or darkness of a color. Many fabrics can be categorized as either light, medium, or dark. If you want your quilt to have sparkle, it is important to use a complete range of value.

You should be able to separate your fabric into three groups: light, medium, and dark or at a minimum, light and dark. There should be an adequate amount of fabric in each group. If not, add to the group(s) that need more. If it is difficult for you to see the difference in value, try squinting your eyes to see the separation of value. With practice this will become second nature.

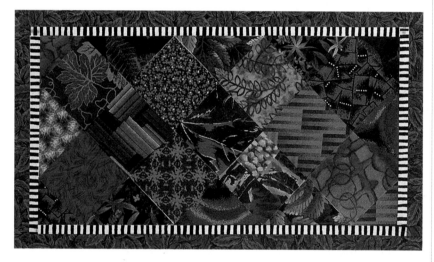

Not enough difference in value.

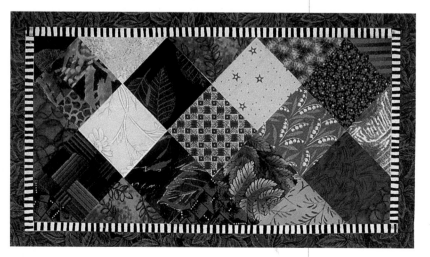

A difference in value makes the quilt more interesting.

Character of Print

"Character of print" refers to the size and scale of the print or the visual texture of a fabric. Most fabrics have character of print. Many new quilters have an idea of what quilting fabrics should look like; often these fabrics are small flower prints. Some quilters get in a rut of purchasing only one print size and style of fabric. It is very important to mix different styles and sizes of prints. If you don't, your quilt could end up looking like it has the chicken pox! Remember, how a fabric looks on the bolt is not how it is going to look after it is cut up. If you have a difficult time seeing a fabric's potential in relationship to character of print, cut a 2" square from the middle of a 3" x 5" index card and hold it up to the fabric in various places.

This will show you how the fabric will look when it is cut up. The fabric's personality, whether you like it or not, will soon be forgotten once it is pieced with its companion fabrics.

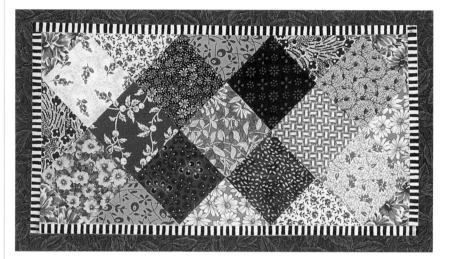

Not enough difference in character of print.

A difference in character of print makes the quilt more interesting.

Color Families

A color family is all of the subtle variations of one color. For example: All blues; from blue-green to blue-violet. All color comes from three basic hues: red, yellow, and blue. From these three (with the addition of black and white), the rest of the color world is made.

When a color is mentioned each of us has our own visual image that comes to mind. For instance, when I mention red, a dark brick red might come to my mind, while you might think of a pinkish red.

Just like fashion, from one season to the next, subtle color change occurs. This year, the blues might all be navy, but next season, they may have a periwinkle hue.

Many times quilters become locked into thinking that all colors need to be perfectly matched; forget that rule. When choosing fabrics for your quilts, it is okay to mix different variations of one color family together. In fact, your quilt will be more interesting if you mix and match. I look for bridge fabrics (page 6) to help make the transition in the diversity of a color family easier.

Not enough variety within the color family.

A greater variety within the color family makes the quilt more interesting.

Color Wheel

The mention of a color wheel can make even the bravest quilter break out in a sweat. There are endless possibilities of color combinations and so many elements to understand. The information looks important on the color wheel and necessary to understand, yet words like hue, tone, tint, and chroma can be confusing at best! I believe that many people are born with the ability to see subtleties in color; it has always been a challenge for me, and I have a degree in art! What we must remember is that in reality we are working with fabrics, which have their own personality, and most likely won't match your predetermined color idea.

So why even bother with a color wheel? There are three basic combinations I use when working with fabric combinations and block placement.

Complementary: A complementary combination uses two colors opposite from each other on the color wheel; for example, red and green. Working with complementary colors provides a rich, dynamic look.

Triadic: If you place an imaginary triangle on top of the color wheel, the colors touched by each corner of the triangle create the combination called a triad. Triads are stimulating and exciting.

Analogous: Colors that appear next to each other on the color wheel are called analogous. This color combination is safe and pleasing.

Once you become familiar with these basic color combinations, you will start to understand the color compositions of fabrics. Many focus fabrics (page 7) contain one of these color combinations—creating different moods. You will be able to take more risks with fabrics by understanding and keeping the basic guidelines of a color wheel in mind.

Pinwheels of Color

This quilt was inspired by Jennifer Sampou's Basics collection by Robert Kaufman Company, complementary, triadic, and analogous color combinations were used for the pinwheel blocks. When it came time to put the blocks together, I again used the color wheel to find appropriate neighbors for each block—complementary, triadic, and analogous. This was a very interesting way to work, and I strongly recommend that you try it sometime.

This quilt is 52" x 48" and consists of one hundred thirty-two 4" Pinwheel blocks. Machine quilted by Paula Reid.

FABRIC GROUPS

Holiday Fabrics

Key to Success:

Use a few holiday prints and many coordinating color and print fabrics.

It is great fun and quite easy to make a holiday quilt. Quilt stores are filled with holiday fabrics; often an entire section may be dedicated to one holiday or another.

Think of your favorite holiday, the one that brings back wonderful memories. Once you have decided which holiday you are going to play with, choose only a few fabrics from that particular holiday section of the store. Then leave that section of the store and pick some coordinating fabrics (fabrics that use the same colors that appear in the holiday fabrics) from other

sections of the store. For example, in my Fourth of July quilt (page 26), I used a few fabrics with stars and patriotic motifs. However, notice how tone-on-tone, sparkle, and other coordinating fabrics have been added. These fabrics give the eyes a place to rest so the quilt doesn't appear too busy/overwhelming. This approach provides a safe way to mix and match unusual fabric combinations using the coordinating colors. If the entire quilt is made using only holiday fabrics, it will be visually confusing. People have different levels of tolerance with regard to busy/overwhelming; what may be too busy for one person may be just right for someone else. By following this formula your quilt will be playful with a sophisticated touch.

Look how busy and confusing this quilt looks using only patriotic fabrics.

The quilt is much more striking with the introduction of other fabrics. These other fabrics give your eyes a place to rest, resulting in a more refined look.

Monochromatic Fabrics

Key to Success:

Use an equal amount of light, medium, and dark prints from one color family.

Working monochromatic means working with only one color. If you are insecure with multiple-color combinations, this color group alleviates those fears, because you are only dealing with only one color. These quilts are stunning. If you feel you have a monochromatic quilt emerging from your soul, you need to start collecting fabric today! To produce an excellent monochromatic quilt you need equal amounts of light, medium, and dark fabrics. As you purchase fabrics for this quilt, you will become acutely aware that most of the fabrics available today are in the medium to medium-dark range. The lights and darks are very difficult to find because they are typically not appealing at first glance. Quilters don't purchase them on impulse, so the quilt stores don't carry these fabrics resulting in the manufacturers not making them. Also, from one season to the next, fabrics have a "look" to them, just like in the fashion industry. For a spectacular quilt, you want to mix the style of prints and color subtleties that arise each season.

Without the full range of value, the quilt lacks interest and sparkle.

Who could resist a bright and sunny yellow quilt. Even though yellow is typically thought of as a light color, a full range of value makes this quilt a success.

Neutral Fabrics

Key to Success:

Use many light to medium beige/brown prints and a few white fabrics.

Choosing fabrics for a neutral quilt is similar to working in the monochromatic color group. The difference is that you are working with fabrics that are typically collected and used as background fabrics. First you must decide on the look you want. Do you want the quilt to be extremely subtle or to have a little punch? If you prefer the soft, subtle look, keep the range of value limited to white to medium beige. If you want a little more punch, push the medium beige range to a soft brown. It is okay to mix white, beige, tan, and gray in this quilt. If this makes you nervous, include a bridge fabric (page 6) that incorporates all the different colors.

Without white the quilt looks muddy and lacks sparkle.

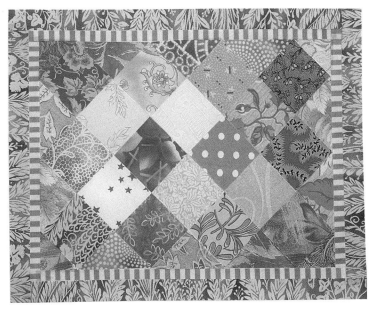

The success of neutral quilts comes from the diversity of print, value, and variety of the basic color family (beige/brown).

The key however is to make sure you use white for sparkle. If you don't, the quilt will look muddy. Sometimes I introduce a few light-colored pastel fabrics with the neutral fabrics. This touch adds interest and another dimension to the quilt. The success of this quilt is based on having a range of value (white, light, and medium) and variety in the character of print (page 9). I've never known anyone who didn't love quilts made in this style, which makes neutral quilts perfect for gifts.

Solid-Colored Fabrics

Key to Success:

Use a full range of light, medium, and dark fabrics.

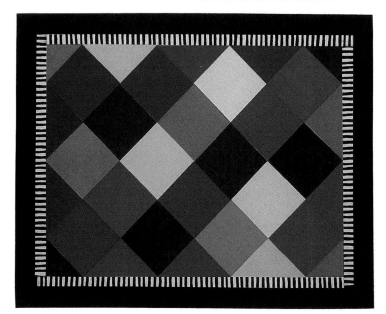

Notice how without the light fabric the quilt looks flat.

If you are intimidated by prints, try working with solid-colored fabrics. The good news is that you only have to deal with solids. The bad news is that every little piecing inaccuracy will show. I reserve solid-colored fabrics for blocks that are easy to assemble and don't have a lot of seams to match. Solid-colored quilts are wonderful if you want your quilting stitches to show. These fabrics showcase all the fancy quilting designs we quilters are so fond of. Value is an important issue when working with solids. The work is done not only by the color, but also by the full range of value: light, medium, and dark. For fun, a stripe can be introduced into the border. Always be willing to take a diversion off the proposed trail; otherwise you will never know what surprises you might find along the journey of quiltmaking.

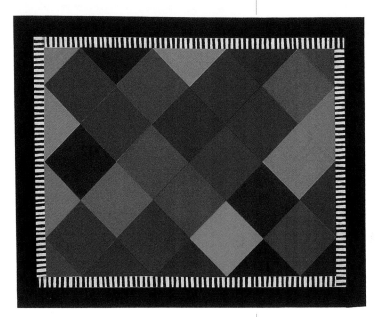

The introduction of very light pastels make this quilt sparkle.

Focus Fabrics

Key to Success:

Use one focus fabric and many coordinating color and print fabrics.

Working with a focus fabric is a sure bet for making a smashing quilt. A focus fabric is a print that dictates the color choices used in the quilt. Typically, focus fabrics are large-scale prints. Pick a fabric that has an interesting color combination and includes variations of each color family (page 10) that appears in the fabric. For example, if the print has leaves, make sure there are several variations of green represented in the leaves. I look for fabrics that combine colors I might not think of putting together or a fabric that forces me to use colors I might ordinarily be uncomfortable working with. Once you have decided on a focus fabric, look carefully and choose several fabrics that represent *all* the colors used in the print, whether you like them or not. You might be surprised at the hidden colors. It is through the process of using colors out of your comfort zone that you will become familiar

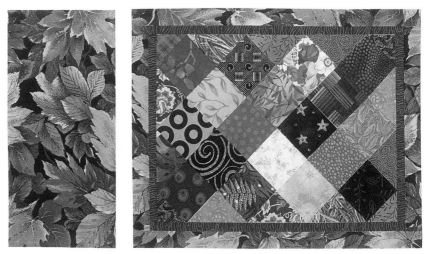

This is a wonderful focus fabric. The green color family has great diversity, and pink has subtly been introduced with the peach.

Try using a focus fabric that has colors that you might not ordinarily be comfortable working with.

with using all colors. The focus fabric may or may not appear on the pieced top. It is simply a color blueprint for the entire quilt. When using a focus fabric, you are letting the fabric designer do the color brainwork for you.

Personality Fabrics

Key to Success:

Use novelty fabrics in combination with calmer fabrics (such as tone-on-tone prints) that reflect the person or place you are trying to capture.

Think of a person or place you would like to document in a quilt.

For a couple of years I purchased any fabrics that reminded me of my daughter Adair. Pigs, stars, hearts, dogs, and cats only begin to tell the story of my daughter. There should be a sense of continuity in the "look" of the fabrics (bright, pastel, graphic, or subdued). I chose to use the brighter fabrics from the quilt store and my fabric collection. Notice that introducing some calmer prints gives the eyes a place to rest. The results are bright, exciting, and a little unpredictable, just like my daughter!

When I was a child we went camping. I can still recall how blue the sky was with its big, fluffy white clouds. The lake was just the right size and

Notice how the fabrics relate to Adair's many traits: she refuses to eat pig, she loves music, and she once considered becoming a marine biologist.

Notice the blue fabrics used for sky and water, sea shell fabrics for the beach, leaf fabrics for the trees, and brown fabrics to match the dirt.

color for kids, the pine trees were enormous, and we would become covered with dirt from head to toe. As I chose fabrics for this project, I used colors and prints that reflected the surroundings; green fabric with leaves, perfect for trees; blue swirly fabric for water. When you work in this format, your fabric color prejudices begin to disappear, because the only thing that matters is whether or not the fabric does the job of telling your story.

Scrap Fabrics

Key to Success:

Use many fabrics and colors to complete 90% of the quilt; fill in with the dominant color that appears for the last 10%.

Even though it's a little scary, this is perhaps the most fun way to explore your fabric stash if you have a little sense of adventure. When making a scrap quilt, you need to make each block its own little independent unit. Don't worry about the block you just made or the one you are going to make next. Just concentrate on one block at a time. As you make each block, hang it on your design wall.

When the quilt is about 90% completed, it's time to pay attention to what is taking form on your design wall. Chances are a certain color will be dominant. It is probably the color you like best. Consider using that color in several of the remaining blocks. It will help pull the whole quilt together. If there are any "screamer" blocks (blocks that really jump out visually), repeat that color at least two more times in other areas of the quilt. I look at my scrap blocks on the design wall for several days to make sure the quilt looks balanced. Often I will use a high-value contrast block in each corner; this helps hold the quilt together. Sometimes these quilts take on lives of their own, but just use the simple tricks mentioned above to rein them back into shape.

Celebrate your fabric selection by working in scrap. Use every color you can think of and let the fun begin.

CARE, STORAGE, DESIGN WALL

Care

As an avid fabric lover and collector, I find that fabrics always seem to pop up in the strangest places. An estate sale might bring riches, or a friend might bless you with her grandmother's sewing supplies. I always accept fabric with a smile. As mentioned before (on page 7), there are different grades of fabric and different fiber combinations. One way to determine how your fabric is going to behave is to prewash it. If it stretches, fades, or falls apart you don't want to use it in your quilt.

For new fabric, there are definitely two different opinions on prewashing. I prewash because I like to know if the fabric is going to shrink, bleed, or act in a mysterious way. In addition, fabric is loaded with chemicals I don't want to handle or breathe. If you like the stiffness of new fabric, consider using spray starch when you press the fabric after washing it and before cutting into it.

If you choose not to prewash, you should at least test your fabric for colorfastness. Cut a two-inch square and put it in boiling water. If the color bleeds into the water, repeat the process. If it no longer bleeds you can use it in your quilt, but you will need to prewash the remainder to feel confident using it. If it continues to discharge color, throw it away; it could ruin your quilt.

Storage

It is important to get organized. There are a million ways to store fabric. However, first and most important, your fabric should be kept out of direct sunlight. The sun can cause serious fading, which can be heartbreaking after all the time and effort you spent collecting the perfect fabrics. Second, your fabric should be easy to access. If it is an effort to pull fabric out to play with, most likely you won't bother.

Each quilter has their own system; it is something that just naturally occurs. As for myself, I removed the doors from my sewing room closet, purchased a spring rod, and made a split curtain to cover the doorway from direct sunlight. My fabric is stored in pull-out wire baskets. This system is a little costly, but the accessibility and ease of use makes it well worth it. When it's time to work, I pull back the curtains and can see my choices through the wire baskets. My fabrics are sorted by color families, with odd fabrics that don't fit into a color family, such as focus, novelty, and plaids, each in their own bin. I fold the fabrics and store them on edge, kind of like a filing box. Only the edge of the fabric is revealed, and I can quickly sort through until I find just the right fabric! Another option is to purchase office supply boxes with lids and sort your fabric in these. You can label the outside of the box with the color family or style of fabric.

Design Wall

Other than my basic sewing supplies and fabric collection, my design wall is probably my most important tool. It gives me the opportunity to evaluate the quilts as they take form. There are several ways to make a design wall. My wall is Cellotex® covered with fleece. Cellotex is an insulation board found in the home improvement stores, that is easy to pin into. The fleece allows me to easily hang and arrange the blocks on the wall without pins. Flannel is also a nice fabric to cover the Cellotex with. If space is an issue, consider purchasing large sheets of foamcore board. Hinge two sheets together on the back with duct tape so they will stand open by themselves, like a book. You can cover the boards with fleece or flannel, or simply pin directly onto the foamcore. When you are done working for the day you can fold the boards together and slip them behind a door.

In addition to a design wall, I use a reducing glass. It looks like a magnifying glass but does the opposite. When you look through it, it creates distance between you and your work . An alternative to a reducing glass is to turn your back to your wall and look at your blocks in a mirror. This too creates distance. When you can view your work from a distance it gives you the opportunity to make fabric decisions that might not seem obvious at close range. For example, are there any areas that are too dark? Or perhaps there is a "screamer" block you were unaware of that needs to be repeated (page 19). A reducing glass or a mirror gives perspective to your work as it hangs on the design wall.

General INSTRUCTIONS

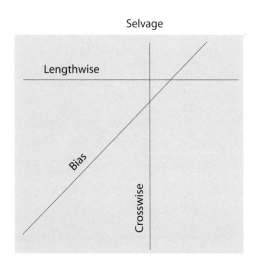

Selvage

Lengthwise

Bias

Crosswise

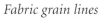

Fabric grain lines

Grain

In quiltmaking, understanding the grain of the fabric is very important. When fabric is produced, the threads are woven in two directions. The two long finished edges of the fabric are called the selvages. Always cut off the selvage edges. If left on, the selvages can cause distortion of the block. This length of the fabric is called the lengthwise grain and has little, if any, stretch. The width of the fabric is called the crosswise grain, and it has a little stretch. The lengthwise or crosswise grain is considered the straight of grain. Diagonally across the grain (no matter what angle) is the bias. Bias edges must be handled, sewn, and pressed with care, since they stretch easily. The cut fabric shape that will be on the outside edge of your finished block should be on the straight of grain whenever possible.

Periodically, a fabric may be printed "off grain." This means that the print of the fabric is not registered properly on the grain. In this case, I compromise by letting the print of the fabric dictate the cut rather than the straight of grain.

Pressing

The arrows on the illustrations indicate which way to press the seams. Pressing the seams in one direction or the other has to do with ease of construction, not the color value of the fabric. In addition to following the arrows, here are a few more things to keep in mind.

1. Press on a firm surface. An ironing board with a single pad is fine.

2. Press your fabric before cutting it. Use spray starch if the fabric seems limp.

3. Once you have cut the shape, never press unless you are moving the seams to one direction or the other. Careless pressing can stretch exposed bias edges.

4. When pressing seams to one side, press the pieced units with the right side up. This helps avoid pressing tucks into the sewn seams.

5. Whenever possible, press seams from the side of the shape that is on the straight of grain. Avoid touching any exposed bias edges with the iron.

While these rules might seem a little picky, developing these habits will serve you well in the long run.

Pinning

I like to pin. As host of "Simply Quilts," I discovered that half the quilting world runs the other direction at the mention of pinning. But I find my results to be much more pleasing when I take the time to pin. Here is how I pin.

1. Use only extra-fine, glasshead pins. They do cost more, but the less expensive "quilting" pins are thick and can cause distortion and unsatisfactory results.

2. When aligning two seams that are pressed in opposite directions, place a pin no more than ⅛" on each side of the seam.

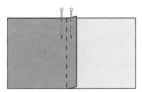

3. If you have two pieces that need to align exactly at a single point, insert the first pin (pin 1) from the wrong side of the pieced shape on the top (exactly at the intersection), into the right side of the pieced unit underneath (exactly at the other intersection). Push the head of the pin tightly into place, and secure pins 2 and 3, no more than ⅛" on each side of pin 1. As you approach the intersection while sewing the seam, remove pin 1 at the last possible second, so that your sewing machine can go right into the hole created by pin 1.

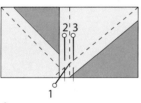

Seam Ripping

Your stitch length should be just long enough so the seam ripper can slide under the stitch. Use a seam ripper with a sharp blade—inexpensive, dull rippers can stretch or ruin the fabric. To pick out a seam, cut every third thread on one side of the pieced unit, then gently lift the thread off the other side of the fabric.

If you have two bias edges sewn together, consider throwing the pieces away and starting over. The chance of stretching the bias edges is almost 100%. If the edges do stretch, the shapes won't align or sew together properly.

Sets

A set refers to the way the blocks are laid out and sewn before the borders are attached. There are two different types of sets used in this book. A straight set is when the blocks are positioned with the sides parallel to the quilt's edge. A diagonal set is when the blocks are set on point and sewn in rows on the diagonal.

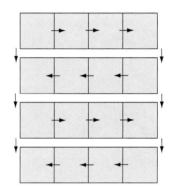

Straight set pressing

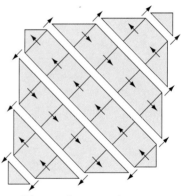

Diagonal set pressing

In both cases, once the blocks are sewn into rows it is best to press the seams of each row alternating directions (e.g., row 1 left, row 2 right, and so on). This will allow you to easily align the seams when sewing the rows together. After the rows are sewn together, press the row seams in one direction.

Borders

If the length of the border is longer than the regular width of fabric (42"), it will be necessary to cut the borders on the fabric's lengthwise grain. When following project instructions, it is wise to cut the borders first, because the length of the fabric may become too short from cutting strips for various pieces in the quilt. When pre-cutting the border strips, always cut the strips a few inches longer than needed.

To determine the *exact* length of the border strips, measure your sewn quilt top across the center from top to bottom and from side to side. Compare your measurements to the project instructions and, if necessary, adjust the cutting measurements of the border strips to the actual length and width of your quilt top.

Backing

Once you have finished your quilt top it's time to consider the backing. Most of the projects in this book are wider than the standard 42"-wide 100% cotton, so it will be necessary to piece the backing. I often use fabric that I wonder why I ever bought (in colors that relate to the quilt) or the focus fabric that wasn't used up. When preparing the backing, here are thoughts to keep in mind.

1. It's OK to use more than one fabric on the pieced back.

2. Never use a sheet or decorator fabric. It has a higher thread count and is difficult to hand quilt through.

3. Always cut off the selvage edges before piecing the fabrics together—the seam might not lie flat.

4. If your quilt has a lot of white in it, use a light-colored fabric on the back. A darker fabric could show through, distorting the colors of the pieced top.

5. Always prewash the backing fabric and piece it a few inches larger on each side than the quilt top, since it can shift during the quilting process.

Batting

For hand quilting, I recommend starting with a low-loft polyester batting. It makes the quilting stitch much easier to learn.

For machine quilting, I recommend you use 100% cotton batting. Make sure you follow the instructions provided if it needs to be prewashed.

Layering

Depending on the size of my project, I either work on a table top (small quilt) or on my non-loop carpet (large quilt). First you must either tape down the backing (table top) or pin using T-pins (carpet). It should be *wrong*-side up and taut.

Carefully unroll the batting and smooth it on top of the backing. Trim the batting to the same size as the backing. Smooth the quilt top over the batting *right*-side up.

Basting
For Hand Quilting

Make a knot in one end of a neutral-colored thread and take large stitches through all three layers.

I like to baste in an approximately 4" grid pattern so that there is an even amount of basting throughout the quilt. Never skimp on this part of the process; your quilt layers may slip and move during the quilting process.

For Machine Quilting

Pin baste every 3" with small safety pins. Pin evenly across the quilt, avoiding areas where the quilting stitches will be sewn.

Quilting

For either hand quilting or machine quilting I have three thoughts to share with you.

1. More is better. Never skimp on the amount of quilting.

2. Treat the pieced surface as a whole. My quilts are often quilted with interesting grids.

3. Use an equal amount of quilting over the entire surface. If you quilt different areas with uneven density your quilt will not only look odd, but also not lie flat.

Binding

The final step in constructing a quilt is the binding. Even here you can celebrate the use of many different fabrics!

1. Trim the batting and backing even with the edges of the quilt top.

2. Cut the strips 2⅛" (or a little wider if you prefer). If necessary piece the strips together with a diagonal seam, trim, and press open.

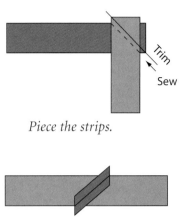

Piece the strips.

Press open.

3. Trim two of the strips the width of the quilt plus 1". Fold and press lengthwise.

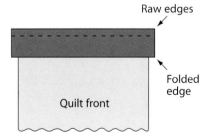

Fold and press.

4. On the top edge of the quilt, align the raw edges of the binding with the raw edge of the quilt. Let the binding extend ½" past the corners of the quilt. Sew using a ¼" seam allowance. Repeat for the bottom edge of the quilt.

Raw edges

Folded edge

Quilt front

Attach binding to front of quilt.

5. Bring the folded edge of the binding over the raw edges of the quilt and slip stitch to the back of the quilt. Trim the ends even with the quilt.

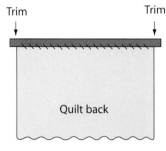

Trim   Trim

Quilt back

Stitch binding and trim

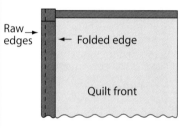

Raw edges

← Folded edge

Quilt front

Attach side binding.

6. For the two sides of the quilt, cut the binding the length of the quilt plus ½" for turning under. Fold over the two ends of the binding to create a finished edge and sew on. Again, turn the folded edge of the binding over the raw edge of the quilt and slip stitch into place.

With the addition of a fabric label on the back to document your effort, your quilt is finished.

Road to California

Key to Success:

Use a few holiday prints and many coordinating color and print fabrics.

This quilt is 49½" x 49½", contains sixteen 9" Road to California blocks, and has forty 4½" Rail Fence blocks for border. Machine quilted by Paula Reid.

Fabric Requirements

Yardage is based on a 42" fabric width. The following instructions give the total yardage needed to complete your quilt. Refer to page 13 to help you choose fabrics.

Blues: ¾ yard

Reds: 1½ yards

Lights: 1¼ yards

Striped inner border: ⅓ yard

Backing: 3 yards

Binding: ⅓ yard

Batting: 53" x 53"

Road to California

The following numbers are for one 9" Road to California block. You will need sixteen.

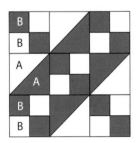

Road to California block

Cutting

Blues

A. Cut two 3⅞" squares, then cut in half diagonally ◻.

B. Cut two 2" squares.

Reds

B. Cut eight 2" squares.

Lights

A. Cut two 3⅞" squares, then cut in half diagonally ◻.

B. Cut ten 2" squares.

Block Assembly

Follow the diagrams as shown for the piecing sequence. The arrows indicate which way to press.

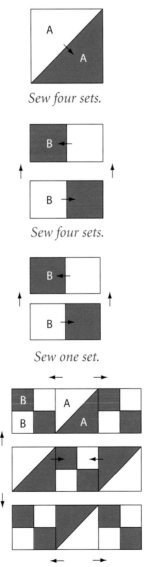

Sew four sets.

Sew four sets.

Sew one set.

Block Assembly

Quilt Top Assembly

1. Arrange your blocks as shown in the diagram. Note that the blocks have been rotated to create a star pattern.

2. Join your blocks in a straight set. Press seams of alternate rows in opposite directions.

Borders

Red Inner Border

1. Cut two 1¼" x 36½" strips.

2. Sew one strip onto each side of the quilt top. Press.

3. Cut two 1¼" x 38" strips.

4. Sew onto the top and bottom of the quilt top. Press.

Striped Inner Border

1. Cut two 2" x 38" strips.

2. Sew one onto each side of the quilt top. Press.

3. Cut two 2" x 41" strips.

4. Sew onto the top and bottom of the quilt top. Press.

Pieced Border

The border is made up of forty 4½" Rail Fence blocks. The following cutting numbers are for one Rail Fence block.

1. Cut three red 2" x 5" rectangles.

2. Piece and press as shown.

Rail Fence block

3. Sew two rows of nine rotated Rail Fence blocks.

4. Sew one onto each side of the quilt top. Press.

5. Sew two rows of eleven rotated Rail Fence blocks.

6. Sew onto the top and bottom of the quilt top. Press.

Celebrate! Your quilt is ready to layer, baste, and quilt. Just in time for your favorite holiday.

Quilt Construction

Variations

A joyous quilt for Christmas

A spooky quilt for Halloween

Double Pinwheel

Key to Success:

**Use an equal
amount of light,
medium, and dark
prints from one
color family.**

*This quilt is 45½" x 51½",
contains forty-two 6" Double
Pinwheel blocks, and has a
3" sawtooth border. Machine
quilted by Paula Reid.*

Fabric Requirements

Yardage is based on a 42" fabric width. The following instructions give the total yardage needed to complete your quilt. Refer to page 14 to help you choose fabrics.

Assorted fabrics (white, light, medium, and dark yellow): 4 yards for blocks and outer border

Inner border: ¼ yard

Backing: 2¾ yards

Binding: ⅓ yard

Batting: 50" x 56"

Double Pinwheel

The following numbers are for one 6" Double Pinwheel block. You will need forty-two.

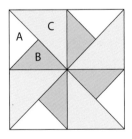

Double Pinwheel block

Cutting

Light Yellow or White

A. Cut one 4¼" square, then cut in half diagonally twice ⊠.

Dark Yellow

B. Cut one 4¼" square, then cut in half diagonally twice ⊠.

Medium Yellow

C. Cut two 3⅞" squares, then cut in half diagonally ◻.

Block Assembly

Follow the diagrams as shown for piecing sequence. The arrows indicate which way to press.

Sew four sets.

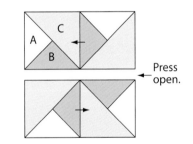

Press open.

Block Assembly

Quilt Top Assembly

1. Arrange your blocks as shown in the diagram.

2. Join your blocks in a straight set. Press seams of alternate rows in opposite directions.

Borders

Inner Border

1. Cut two 2" x 42½" strips.

2. Sew one strip onto each side of the quilt top. Press.

3. Cut two 2" x 39½" strips.

4. Sew onto the top and bottom of the quilt top. Press.

Outer Border

1. Cut twenty-nine 3⅞" squares from the light and medium fabrics, then cut in half diagonally ◻.

2. Cut two 3½" squares from the light and medium fabrics.

3. Cut twenty-nine 3⅞" squares from the medium and dark fabrics, then cut in half diagonally ◻.

4. Sew fifty-eight half-square triangle units. Press toward the darker fabric.

Half-square triangle unit

5. Sew two rows of thirteen half-square triangle units. Sew onto the top and bottom of the quilt top. Press.

6. Sew two rows of sixteen half-square triangle units and add one square to opposite ends. Sew one onto each side of the quilt top. Press.

Congratulations!

Aren't monochromatic quilts wonderful? Your quilt is ready to layer, baste, and quilt.

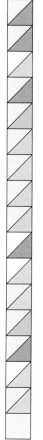

Quilt Construction

Variations

Green, ideal for the outdoor person in your life.

Pink, perfect for any little girl.

Snail's Trail Variation

This quilt is 61½" x 69½" and contains forty-two 8" Snail's Trail blocks. Machine quilted by Paula Reid.

Fabric Requirements

Yardage is based on a 42" fabric width. The following instructions give the total yardage needed to complete your quilt. Refer to page 15 to help you choose fabrics.

Assorted fabrics (white through beige): 3 yards

Inner border: ⅓ yard

Outer border: 1¾ yards

Backing: 3¾ yards

Binding: ½ yard

Batting: 66" x 74"

Snail's Trail Variation

Sort the fabric into piles of light and dark. The following numbers are for one 8" Snail's Trail block. You will need forty-two.

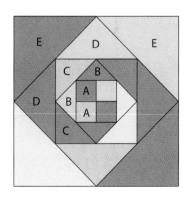

Snail's Trail block

Cutting

Lights

A. Cut two 1½" squares.

B. Cut one 2¼" squares, then cut in half diagonally ◁.

C. Cut one 2⅞" square, then cut in half diagonally ◁.

D. Cut one 3¾" square, then cut in half diagonally ◁.

E. Cut one 4⅞" square, then cut in half diagonally ◁.

Darks

A. Cut two 1½" squares.

B. Cut one 2¼" square, then cut in half diagonally ◁.

C. Cut one 2⅞" square, then cut in half diagonally ◁.

D. Cut one 3¾" square, then cut in half diagonally ◁.

E. Cut one 4⅞" square, then cut in half diagonally ◁.

Block Assembly

Follow the diagrams as shown for piecing sequence. The arrows indicate which way to press.

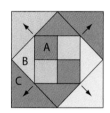
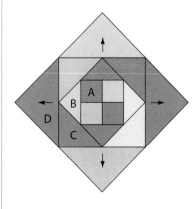
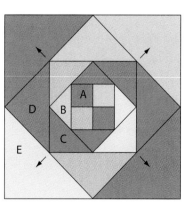

Block Assembly

Quilt Top Assembly

1. Arrange your blocks as shown in the diagram.

2. Join your blocks in a straight set. Press seams of alternate rows in opposite directions.

Borders

Inner Border

1. Cut six 1½" x 42" strips. Sew end-to-end into one strip. Cut two 56½" lengths for the side borders and two 50½" lengths for the top and bottom borders.

2. Sew side borders onto the quilt top. Press.

3. Sew the top and bottom borders onto the quilt top. Press.

Outer Border

1. From lengthwise grain, cut two 6" x 58½" strips.

2. Sew one strip onto each side of the quilt top. Press.

3. From lengthwise grain, cut two 6" x 61½" strips.

4. Sew onto the top and bottom of the quilt top. Press.

Good job! Note that this is an unusual set for Snail's Trail, but it is very effective in neutrals. Your quilt is now ready to layer, baste, and quilt.

Quilt Construction

Variations

Using a greater range of value gives the pattern a more distinct look.

The look becomes much more subtle and soft with less value range.

Churn Dash

Key to Success:

**Use a full range of
light, medium, and
dark fabrics.**

*This quilt is 55⅞" x 55⅞" and
contains twenty-five 6" Churn
Dash blocks. Machine quilted
by Paula Reid.*

Fabric Requirements

Yardage is based on a 42" fabric width. The following instructions give the total yardage needed to complete your quilt. Refer to page 16 to help you choose fabrics.

Assorted solid-colored fabrics: 1 yard for blocks and cornerstones

Black: 4 yards for background, sashing, and outer border

Pink inner border: ¼ yard

Striped inner border: ¼ yard

Backing: 3⅓ yards

Binding: ⅜ yard

Batting: 60" x 60"

Churn Dash

The following numbers are for one 6" Churn Dash block. You will need twenty-five.

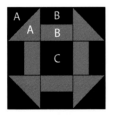

Churn Dash block

Cutting

Solid-colored fabrics

A. Cut two 2⅞" squares, then cut in half diagonally ◺.

B. Cut four 1½" x 2½" rectangles.

Black

From the lengthwise grain, cut two 47⅞" strips for the side borders and two 6" x 55⅞" strips for the top and bottom borders. Set aside for the outer borders.

A. Cut two 2⅞" squares, then cut in half diagonally ◺.

B. Cut four 1½" x 2½" rectangles.

C. Cut one 2½" square.

If you would like to cut the black fabric for all of the blocks at once, rather than for one block (given above):

A. Cut four 2⅞"-wide strips. From the strips cut fifty 2⅞" squares, then cut in half diagonally ◺.

B. Cut seven 1½"-wide strips. From the strips, cut one hundred 1½" x 2½" rectangles.

C. Cut two 2½"-wide strips. From the strips, cut twenty-five 2½" squares.

Sashing

Cut eleven 1½" x 42" strips. Then cut the strips into sixty-four 1½" x 6½" rectangles for sashing strips.

Cut forty 1½" squares for corner stones.

Block Assembly

Follow the diagrams as shown for piecing sequence. The arrows indicate which way to press.

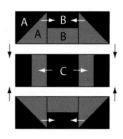

Block Assembly

Quilt Top Assembly

This quilt is a diagonal set with sashing and cornerstones.

1. Lay out the blocks, sashing, and cornerstones as shown.

2. Sew into diagonal rows as shown. Press.

3. Cut three 11⅛" squares, then cut in half diagonally twice ⊠ for the side triangles.

4. Cut two 6⅝" squares, then cut in half diagonally ◺ for the corner triangles.

5. Sew the side and corner triangles onto the rows. Press.

6. Join the rows. Press.

Sew into rows.

Borders

Pink Inner Border

1. Cut five 1½" strips. Sew end-to-end into one strip. Cut two 41⅜" lengths for the side borders and two 43⅜" lengths for the top and bottom borders.

2. Sew the side borders onto the quilt top. Press.

3. Sew the top and bottom borders onto the quilt top. Press.

Striped Inner Border

1. Cut five 1¼" strips. Sew end-to-end into one strip. Cut two 43⅜" lengths for the side borders and two 44⅞" lengths for the top and bottom borders.

2. Sew the side borders onto the quilt top. Press.

3. Sew the top and bottom borders onto the quilt top. Press.

Outer Border

1. Sew the side borders onto the quilt top. Press.

2. Sew the top and bottom borders onto the quilt top. Press.

Variations

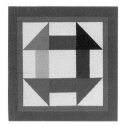

Bright with a white background gives a crisp, fresh look.

Softening the color gives an updated, peaceful appearance.

Hooray! Your solid fabric quilt is finished. Your quilt is now ready to layer, baste, and quilt.

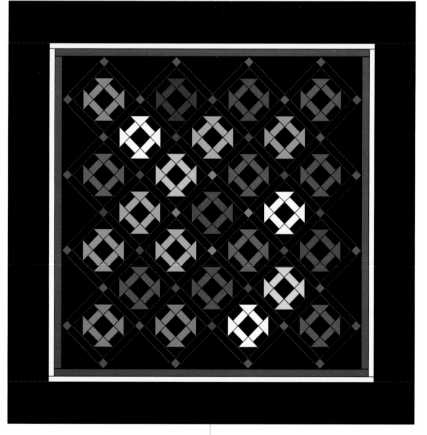

Quilt Construction

37

Baskets

Focus Fabrics

Key to Success:

Use one focus fabric and many coordinating color and print fabrics.

This quilt is 54" x 54" and contains forty-one 6" Basket blocks. Machine quilted by Paula Reid.

Fabric Requirements

Yardage is based on a 42" fabric width. The following instructions give the total yardage needed to complete your quilt. Refer to page 17 to help you choose fabrics.

Assorted fabrics (lights, mediums, and darks): 3⅜ yards for baskets and background

Inner border: ⅓ yard

Outer border and setting triangles: 1⅝ yards

Backing: 3⅓ yards

Binding: ⅜ yard

Batting: 58" x 58"

Basket

The following numbers are for one 6" Basket block. You will need forty-one.

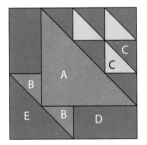

Basket block

Cutting

Basket

A: Cut one 5⅜" square, then cut in half diagonally ◻.

B: Cut one 2⅜" square, then cut in half diagonally ◻.

Flowers

C: Cut two 2⅜" squares, then cut in half diagonally ◻.

Background

C: Cut three 2⅜" squares, then cut in half diagonally ◻.

D: Cut two 2" x 3½" rectangles.

E: Cut one 3⅞" square, then cut in half diagonally ◻.

Block Assembly

Follow the diagram as shown for piecing sequence. The arrows indicate which way to press.

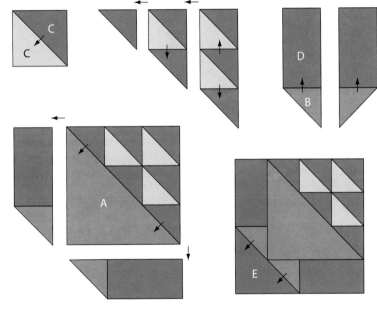

Block Assembly

Quilt Top Assembly

1. From the lengthwise grain, cut two 5" x 45" strips for the top and bottom borders and two strips 5" x 54" for the side borders.

2. Cut four 9¾" squares, then cut in half diagonally twice ⊠ for the side triangles.

3. Cut two 5⅛" squares, then cut in half diagonally ◻ for the corner triangles.

4. Lay out your blocks as shown. Note that they are set on point.

5. Join the pieced blocks and the side and corner triangles in a diagonal set. Press the seams of alternate rows in opposite directions.

Borders

Inner Border

1. Cut five 1½" x 42" strips. Sew end-to-end into one strip. Cut two 43" lengths for the top and bottom borders and two 45" lengths for the side borders.

2. Sew the top and bottom borders onto the quilt top. Press.

3. Sew the side borders onto the quilt top. Press.

Outer Border

1. Sew the top and bottom borders onto the quilt top. Press.

2. Sew the side borders onto the quilt top. Press.

Good job! Your beautiful basket quilt is ready to layer, baste, and quilt.

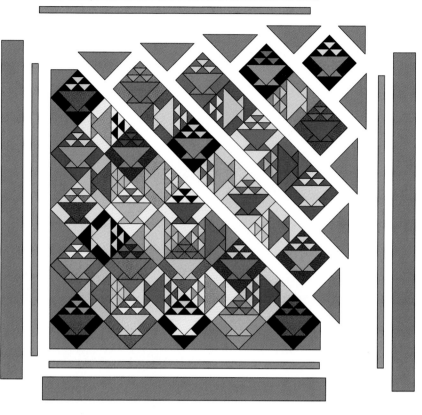

Quilt Construction

Variations

Choose fabrics to create a soft romantic look.

Create a child's quilt with a bright cheery fabric.

Cross Roads

Personality Fabrics

Key to Success:

Use novelty, texture, and calmer fabrics (such as tone-on-tone prints) that reflect the person or place you are trying to capture.

This quilt is 49" x 55" and contains forty-two 6" Cross Roads blocks. Machine quilted by Paula Reid.

Fabric Requirements

Yardage is based on a 42" fabric width. The following instructions give the total yardage needed to complete your quilt. Refer to page 18 to help you choose fabrics.

Assorted prints: 3 yards

First inner border: ⅓ yard

Second inner border: ⅓ yard

Outer border: 1½ yards

Backing: 3 yards

Binding: ⅜ yard

Batting: 53" x 59"

Cross Roads

The following numbers are for one 6" Cross Roads block. You will need forty-two.

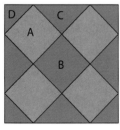

Cross Roads block

Cutting

A. Cut four 2⅝" squares.

B. Cut one 2⅝" square.

C. Cut one 4¼" square, then cut in half diagonally twice ⊠.

D. Cut two 2⅜" squares, then cut in half diagonally ◺.

Block Assembly

Follow the diagram as shown for piecing sequence. The arrows indicate which way to press.

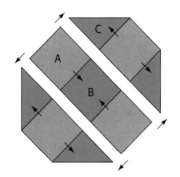

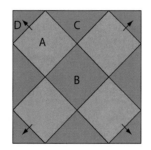

Block Assembly

Quilt Top Assembly

1. Arrange your blocks as shown in the diagram.

2. Join your blocks in a straight set. Press seams open. (Whenever there are six seams or more converging in one place, it is okay to press the seam open.)

Borders
First Inner Border

1. Cut two 1½" x 42½" strips.

2. Sew one strip onto each side of the quilt top. Press.

3. Cut two 1½" x 38½" strips.

4. Sew onto the top and bottom of the quilt top. Press.

Second Inner Border

1. Cut three 1¼" x 42" strips. Sew end-to-end into one strip. Cut two 44½" lengths for the side borders.

2. Sew one strip onto each side of the quilt top. Press.

3. Cut two 1¼" x 40" strips.

4. Sew onto the top and bottom of the quilt top. Press.

Outer Border

1. From lengthwise grain, cut two 5" x 46" strips.

2. Sew one strip onto each side of the quilt top. Press.

3. From lengthwise grain, cut two 5" x 49" strips.

4. Sew onto the top and bottom of the quilt top. Press.

Congratulations!

What an adventure. These quilts are a little tricky, but well worth the time. Your quilt is now ready to layer, baste, and quilt.

Quilt Construction

Variations

I collected cherry fabrics which bring back dear memories of my grandparents' farm in Door County, Wisconsin.

These fabrics represent many of my son Joey's favorite things and hobbies.

Hearts

Scrap Fabrics

Key to Success:

Use many fabrics and colors to complete 90% of the quilt; fill in with the dominant color that appears for the last 10%.

This quilt is 50" x 50" and contains seventy-seven 4½" Heart blocks. Machine quilted by Paula Reid.

Fabric Requirements

Yardage is based on a 42" fabric width. The following instructions give the total yardage needed to complete your quilt. Refer to page 19 to help you choose fabrics.

Seventy-seven pairs of 8" squares of fabric for hearts and backgrounds

Backing: 3 yards

Binding: ⅓ yard

Batting: 54" x 54"

Tagboard: 3½" square

Heart

The following numbers are for one 4½" Heart block. You will need seventy-seven.

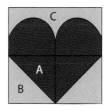

Heart block

Cutting
Heart Top

Trace and cut one template of the heart top from tagboard. Mark the dot on the template.

A. Cut one 3⅛" square from heart fabric, then cut in half diagonally ◺. Using the template, trace two mirror images of the heart top on the wrong side of the remaining fabric.

Cut ¼" around the drawn line of the arc. Mark the stop sewing dot on the wrong side of the fabric. Leave ⅜"–½" at the straight bottom edge of the shape.

Heart Bottom and Background

B. Cut one 3⅛" square, then cut in half diagonally ◺.

C. Cut one 2¾" x 5" rectangle.

Filler Squares and Border

Cut all of the leftover heart and background fabric into 2¾" squares. Set aside. You will cut more than the 176 squares needed. Save the remainder for another project.

Block Assembly

Follow the diagram as shown for piecing sequence. The arrows indicate which way to press.

1. Sew the triangles together. Press.

Press open.

2. Sew to the dot and backstitch. Press seam open.

sew to dot

3. Knot your thread and sew a gathering stitch ⅛" from the raw edge on each heart top, starting from the center and working to the outer edge. Leave a couple of inches for thread to pull the gathers.

Trim ¼" from sew line.

4. Line up the template to the drawn line and gather the stitches around the template. With the template in place, press to form the desired arc shape. Remove template and repeat on the other half of the heart top.

5. Trim the base line of the heart top to ¼".

6. Center the heart top on the rectangle, right side up. Pin if necessary. Piece and press as shown.

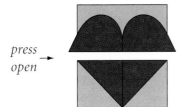

press open →

7. Appliqué the heart top to the background by hand or machine.

8. Follow the block assembly instructions above and make the rest of the heart blocks.

Quilt Top Assembly

1. Arrange the Heart blocks in a pleasing manner, staggering each vertical row by half a block. You will have four rows of eight and five rows of nine.

2. Sew into vertical rows. Press.

3. Examine the Heart blocks and note which colors are most commonly used. From the previously cut 2¾" squares in these colors, choose sixteen squares. This helps give the quilt color continuity.

4. Add two squares to the top and bottom of the short rows.

5. Sew the rows together. Press.

Border

1. From the previously cut 2¾" squares, choose one hundred sixty squares.

2. Arrange the squares in a pleasing manner.

3. Sew eighteen pairs of squares for the top and bottom border. Press.

4. Sew twenty-two pairs of squares for the side borders. Press.

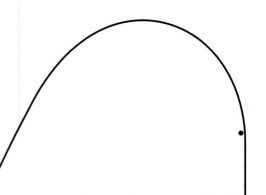

Template pattern

Quilt Construction

Congratulations!

It was a little challenging, but hopefully, fun! This is a wonderful way to become reacquainted with your fabric collection or an excellent project for a fabric exchange. Your quilt is now ready to layer, baste, and quilt.

About theAuthor

According to Alex Anderson's "mission statement," her goal is to inspire and educate as many quilters as possible. Luckily, Alex is in a position to do just that. As host of HGTV's "Simply Quilts," she is well-known to the quilting community. Her award-winning quilts have been displayed at shows around the country for more than 20 years, and widely published in books and magazines

She's also a very popular quilting teacher. "There are so many different ways to do things! Once students have mastered the basics, they're free to go their own way and develop their own personal style. But there's nothing I love more than introducing people to the fundamentals of quiltmaking."

Alex describes her style of quiltmaking as "innovative-traditional." Her roots in the fine arts—she has a degree in art from San Francisco State University—and her deep appreciation for the work of quilters from past centuries have inspired her particular focus on fabric and color relationships along with traditional quilting designs.

Alex lives in northern California, with her family. *Fabric Shopping with Alex Anderson* is her 6th book from C&T Publishing and the 4th title in her Quilting Basics series.

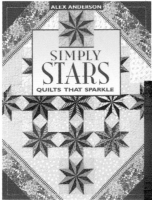

Other Books by Alex Anderson

Win a $500 Fabric Shopping Spree from C&T Publishing, Inc!

Rules for the Drawing

Prize to be Awarded

1. One $500 Fabric Shopping Spree at your favorite quilt shop, fabric store, mail-order catalog, or on-line shop.

2. C&T will present a check for $500 (payable in U.S. dollars) to one retailer (as stated in 1. above) of your choice. You will be able to purchase any amounts and combinations of fabrics up to a total retail value of $500.

Eligibility

1. No purchase of any kind is required to enter.

2. One entry per person.

3. The contest is open to anyone in the United States except employees of C&T Publishing Inc., their family members, and those excluded as stated within the Rules for the Drawing.

4. By submitting an entry, winner agrees to the use of his or her name, city and state, and photograph for advertising/publicity purposes without compensation.

5. Winner must agree to promptly sign an Affidavit of Eligibility. Winner's chosen retailer must promptly sign a receipt for the $500 check.

6. All entries become the property of C&T Publishing Inc. and the contest judge.

7. Contest is void in New York, Rhode Island, Florida, and where otherwise prohibited by law.

How to Enter

1. Mail-In Entries: Write the following information on an 8½" x 11" sheet of paper: your name, complete mailing address, telephone number, name of your favorite quilt shop, and if available, your fax number and e-mail address. Send to Fabric Shopping Spree Entry, c/o C&T Publishing, Inc., 1651 Challenge Drive, Concord, CA 94520. Mail-in entries must be postmarked no later than November 30, 2000 and received no later than 5:00p.m. Pacific Standard Time December 8, 2000.

2. Fax Entries: Fax your entry to C&T Publishing, Inc. at 925-677-0373. Include the words "Fabric Shopping Spree Entry," your name, complete mailing address, telephone number, name of your favorite quilt shop, your fax number, and if available, your e-mail address. Faxed entries must be received no later than 5:00 p.m. Pacific Standard Time, November 30, 2000.

3. E-mail Entries: E-mail your entry to ctinfo@ctpub.com. Include the words "Fabric Shopping Spree Entry" in the Subject box, your name, complete mailing address, telephone number, name of your favorite quilt shop, your e-mail address, and if available, your fax number. E-mail entries must be received no later than 5:00 p.m. Pacific Standard Time, November 30, 2000.

4. Internet Entries: Visit C&T's web site, http://www.ctpub.com/fabricspree.html, where an entry form will be provided. Include your name, complete mailing address, telephone number, name of your favorite quilt shop, and if available, your fax number and e-mail address on the Fabric Shopping Spree Entry form. Internet entries must be received no later than 5:00p.m. Pacific Standard Time, November 30, 2000.

5. Contest begins April 1, 2000, 12:01 a.m. Pacific Standard Time and ends November 30, 2000, 5:00 p.m. Pacific Standard Time.

6. Not responsible for late, lost, incomplete, or illegible entries.

7. Entries must be complete to win.

Awarding of Prize

1. One winner will be selected by the contest judge at random from all entries received by the deadline dates as described above. Winner need not be present to win.

2. Decision of the contest judge is final. Contest judge is unaffiliated with the sponsor, C&T Publishing, Inc.

3. No substitution in prize will be allowed, and prize may not be redeemed for cash or other consideration.

4. Winner will be notified by telephone or mail by December 15, 2000.

5. Prize will be awarded and distributed on or before December 30, 2000.

6. Odds of winning are incalculable and depend on the number of eligible entries received by mail, fax, Internet, or e-mail by the deadline date.

7. Winner is solely responsible for all taxes where applicable. Winner is solely responsible for any costs related to visiting or ordering from their chosen retailer.

8. For a notice of contest winner, send a self-addressed stamped envelope to the contest sponsor: Fabric Shopping Spree Winner, C&T Publishing, Inc., 1651 Challenge Drive, Concord, CA 94520, or visit our website at http://www.ctpub.com.